COUNSELING TECHNIQUES:

An Outline & Overview

Frederick D. Harper, Ph.D.
Howard University

Gail C. Bruce-Sanford, Ph.D.
George Mason University

Douglass Publishers, Alexandria, VA 22302

Published by:
Douglass Publishers
P.O. Box 3270
Alexandria, VA 22302

Printed in the United States of America

ISBN 0-935392-04-1

Copyright © (1989) by Douglass Publishers

First Printing, March 1989

CONTENTS

ABOUT THE AUTHORS

Dr. Frederick D. Harper is a Professor of Counseling Psychology in the School of Education at Howard University.

Dr. Gail C. Bruce-Sanford is a Counselor in the Counseling Center at George Mason University.

SECTION 1

Counseling Concepts

001   **DEFINITIONS OF COUNSELING**

Counseling is a concept and thus has many definitions. Although all definitions of counseling have common properties, they tend to vary in focus. That is, a definition may be slanted toward a certain theory, counseling setting, client population, or problem area. The definitions that follow demonstrate such commonalities and variations:

1. Counseling is "a relationship in which one person endeavors to help another to understand and solve his adjustment problems," i.e., adjustment in terms of educational, vocational, and personal-social concerns (English & English, 1958).

2. Counseling is the "psychological process by which a professional person helps a relatively normal client to explore, understand, and accept behavior so that future behavioral choices can be made, particularly those of an educational or vocational nature" (Cottle, 1973).

3. Counseling is a process involving a special kind of relationship between a person who asks for help with a psychological problem (the client or patient) and a person who is trained to provide that help (the counselor or therapist). (See Patterson, 1986.)

4. Counseling is a one-to-one relationship between counselor and client which focuses on rational planning, problem-solving, decision-making, and situational pressures as related to the client's daily living (Brammer & Shostrom, 1982).

5. Counseling is a relaxed, safe, and facilitative relationship in which an incongruent, disorganized, and troubled person moves toward becoming open, integrated, secure, and fully functioning (Rogers, 1961).

6. Counseling is "a professional relationship wherein a counselor helps one or more persons to develop, resolve a problem, and/or gain greater understanding about a concern" (Harper, 1981).

References

Brammer, L.M., & Shostrom, E.L. (1982). Therapeutic psychology (4th ed.). Englewood Cliffs: Prentice-Hall.

Cottle, W.C. (1973). Beginning counseling practicum. New York: Grune & Stratton.

English, H.B., & English, A.C. (1958). A comprehensive dictionary of psychological and psychiatric terms. New York: McKay.

Harper, F.D. (1981). Dictionary of counseling techniques and terms. Alexandria, VA: Douglass.

Patterson, C.H. (1986). Theories of counseling and psychotherapy (4th ed.). New York: Harper & Row.

Rogers, C.R. (1961). On becoming a person. Boston: Houghton Mifflin.

Suggested Readings

Beck, C.E. (1971). Philosophical guidelines for counseling (2nd ed.). Dubuque: Wm. C. Brown.

Kottler, J.A., & Brown, R.W. (1985). Introduction to therapeutic counseling. Monterey, CA: Brooks/Cole.

Malcolm, D.D. (1968). On becoming a counselor. Journal of Counseling & Development (formerly the Personnel & Guidance Journal), 46, 673-676.

---

002   COUNSELING COMPARED WITH PSYCHOTHERAPY

The question here is, "Is there a difference between counseling and psychotherapy?" One view is that there is no significant difference between the two processes, while a second posits that counseling and psychotherapy differ in terms of (a) the population served, (b) nature or content of the problem, (c) severity of the problem, and (d) setting in which the process occurs. Some of these views follow:

Views of Counseling Versus Psychotherapy

1. Patterson (1986) assumes there is no "essential" difference between the concepts of "counseling" and "psychotherapy."

2. Warters (1964) takes the view that "counseling" and "psychotherapy" are difficult to distinguish in terms of differences; however, she notes that counseling deals with problems that are less severe than those of psychotherapy.

3. Corey (1986) differentiates "counseling" from "psychotherapy" in describing that counseling is short-term, focuses on minor problems, assists one to remove "blocks to growth," and helps one to discover inner resources for effective living; wherein psychotherapy focuses more on unconscious processes, personality-structure changes, and intensive self-understanding. (Corey uses the two concepts together in the same breath as well as interchangeably.)

4. Tyler (1969) cites counseling to be more concerned with role problems while psychotherapy deals more with intrapsychic conflict (i.e., the interpersonal versus the intrapersonal).

5. Morse & Watson (1977) define psychotherapy in terms of an interaction between a patient and a therapist wherein the patient seeks psychological help and the therapist structures the interaction using psychological principles which aid the patient to acquire control over his or her life via changing thoughts, feelings, and actions.

Summary of Similarities and Differences

The following is a list of key similarities and differences between the two concepts:

SIMILARITIES
- Counseling and psychotherapy can both be classified as helping professions.
- Both involve a professional person trained in psychological principles and techniques.

- The goal of both counseling and psychotherapy is "positive change" in human behavior.
- Both counseling and psychotherapy involve, in the main, the practice and use of the same techniques and theories.

DIFFERENCES

- Counseling is much more likely to be short-term (fewer counseling sessions).
- Counseling is more likely to involve clients with adjustment problems, while psychotherapy frequently deals with serious behavior disorders.
- Counseling is more prone to focus on interpersonal conflict, wherein psychotherapy more often involves intrapsychic conflict.
- The psychotherapist is more likely to be trained as a clinical psychologist or psychiatrist and is more likely to use the term "patient" instead of "client" or "counselee."

As a final note to this topic, it may be observed that counseling, psychotherapy, and therapy are often used interchangeably in the professional literature.

References

Corey, G. (1986). Theory and practice of counseling and psychotherapy (3rd ed.). Monterey, CA: Brooks/Cole.

Morse, S.J., & Watson, R.I. (Eds.). (1977). Psychotherapies: A comparative casebook. New York: Holt, Rinehart & Winston.

Patterson, C.H. (1986). Theories of counseling and psychotherapy (4th ed.). New York: Harper & Row

Tyler, L.E. (1969). The work of the counselor (3rd ed.). New York: Appleton-Century-Crofts.

Warters, J. (1964). Techniques of counseling (2nd ed.). New York: McGraw-Hill.

---

003   **GOALS OF COUNSELING**

Goals of counseling are frequently discussed in terms of the following dimensions and criteria:

DIMENSIONS
- Specific goals versus general goals
- Short-Term goals versus long-term goals
- Counseling goals versus psychotherapy goals

CRITERIA (of appropriate goals of counseling)
- Are the goals observable (in terms of outcomes)?
- Are the goals measurable?
- Are the goals desirable for the client and society?
- Are the goals attainable or realistic?

Moreover, goals of counseling may differ according to (a) counseling setting, (b) counseling or treatment modality employed, (c) nature of the client's problem, (d) theory of counseling employed (Table 1), and (e) models of mental health (Table 2).

Goals Defined by Counseling Setting

EDUCATIONAL COUNSELING   (educational decision-making, improved academic performance)

PLACEMENT COUNSELING   (placement in appropriate job or training situation)

VOCATIONAL COUNSELING   (vocational adjustment, decision about a career or occupation)

MARRIAGE COUNSELING   (marital adjustment, resolution of specific marital problems, decision-making about future of marriage)

DRUG/ALCOHOLISM COUNSELING   (abstention, drug-free state, knowledge about drugs and/or alcohol)

CONSUMER COUNSELING   (effective decision-making about buying, sound financial management and planning)

ACADEMIC ADVISEMENT   (appropriate decisions about academic courses)

Goals Defined by Counseling/Treatment Modality

OUTREACH COUNSELING   (establish rapport in client's natural setting, discover concerns of client)

GROUP COUNSELING   (adjustment, prevention of problems, self-improvement, interpersonal effectiveness)

GROUP GUIDANCE (provide information for decision-making and the prevention of problems)

GROUP PSYCHOTHERAPY (awareness, resolution of conflict, insight, self-understanding)

COMMON-PROBLEM GROUP (resolution of a problem that is common to all members of a therapeutic group)

INDIVIDUAL COUNSELING (personal adjustment, decision-making, prevention of problems, interpersonal effectiveness)

INDIVIDUAL PSYCHOTHERAPY (resolution of intrapersonal conflict, insight, personal adjustment, resolution of serious personality disorders)

Goals Defined by Client's Problem

Specific goals of counseling are often established as based on the particular presenting problem or need of the client. In general, the specific goal is stated in terms of **resolving**, **minimizing**, or **preventing** particular behavior problems such as those listed below (e.g., Krumboltz & Thoresen, 1976; Hardy & Cull, 1974; Morse & Watson, 1977):

Anxiety	Alcoholism	Enuresis
Depression	Sexual inadequacy	Encopresis
Stress	Drug abuse	Shyness
Insomnia	Dependency (co-dependency)	Indecisiveness
Phobias	Poor personal appearance	Aggression
Grief	Low self-esteem	Cigarette smoking
Guilt feeling	Social inadequacy	Irresponsibility
Exhibitionism	Marital conflict	Poor study habits
Obesity	Racial bias or conflict	Nightmares
Child abuse	Study problems	Sex bias
Tardiness	Identity problems	Procrastination
Loneliness	Temper tantrum	Unemployment
Family problems	Lack of self-confidence	Moral conflict

Goals Defined by Counseling Theory

Goals of counseling are defined differently depending upon the theoretical orientation of the counselor or the specific theory of counseling and psychotherapy in question. Table 1 presents the various, popular theories of counseling and psychotherapy with their stated goals for change in the client.

Table 1

Goals by Theories of Counseling and Psychotherapy

Theories	Goals
Actualizing Therapy	Responsibility, freedom, awareness, self-fulfillment
Behavior Therapy	Change in a specific behavioral response, change in the frequency of a response
Client-Centered Therapy	Self-Direction, openness, congruence, improved self-structure, fully-functioning person
Eclectic Counseling	Integration of experience and functioning, consciousness
Existential Counseling	Meaning in life, freedom to act, freedom to choose, self-actualization, reduced anxiety
Gestalt Therapy	Awareness, acceptance of responsibility, integration
Psychoanalysis	Insight, reduction in anxiety, resolution of conflict
Rational-Emotive Therapy	Rational thinking, logical thinking, happiness, elimination of anxiety, responsibility, rational living
Reality Therapy	Responsibility, positive self-worth, meeting basic human needs
Systematic Counseling	Attainable learning objectives, responsibility, positive change in behavior
Trait-and-Factor Counseling (or Trait-Factor Counseling)	Social adjustment, problem solving, appropriate and realistic decision-making
Transactional Analysis	Improved transactions, more active "adult" (a la parent, child, adult), resolution of interpersonal and intrapersonal conflict

Goals Defined as Models of Mental Health

General or broader goals of counseling have been defined in terms of traditional models of positive mental health. Some of these models are delineated in Table 2 by name of model, author(s) of model, and description of model.

References

Allport, G.W. (1961). Pattern and growth in personality. New York: Holt, Rinehart & Winston.

Blocher, D.H. (1974). Developmental counseling (2nd ed.). New York: Ronald Press.

Combs, A., & Snygg, D. (1959). Individual behavior (2nd ed.). New York: Harper & Row.

Hardy, R.E., & Cull, J.G. (1974). Group counseling and therapy techniques in special settings. Springfield, IL: Charles C. Thomas.

Krumboltz, J.D., & Thoresen, C.E. (Eds.). (1976). Counseling methods. New York: Holt, Rinehart & Winston.

Maslow, A. (1970). Motivation and personality (2nd ed.). New York: Harper & Row.

Morse, S.J., & Watson, R.I. (Eds.). (1977). Psychotherapies: A comparative casebook. New York: Holt, Rinehart & Winston.

Rogers, C.R. (1951). Client-Centered therapy. Boston: Houghton Mifflin.

Shoben, C.J. (1957). Toward a concept of the normal personality. American Psychologist, 12, 183-189.

004　　　　　　　**DEFINITIONS AND NATURE OF "THEORY"**

All disciplines or bodies of knowledge, including the field of counseling, have their own theories which explain phenomena. The following discussion provides background information in regards to what a theory is and what it does.

Definitions of Theory

- A theory is a "cluster of relevant assumptions systematically related to each other" as well as a set of empirical definitions (Hall & Lindzey, 1978).

- A theory is a set of interrelated and internally consistent assumptions from which hypotheses are derived and made testable by the use of operational

Table 2

Models of Mental Health as General Goals for Counseling

Models of Mental Health	Authors of Models	Descriptions of Models
The Self-Actualizing Person	Abraham Maslow (1970)	The **self-actualizing person** has realistic perceptions; accepts self/others; is spontaneous; focuses on external problems; has a tendency to prefer privacy; has consistent appreciation of experiences; is capable of mystic/ecstatic feelings; identifies with humankind; has effective interpersonal relationships (including cross-cultural relationships); is independent; focuses on ends rather than means; has a philosophical sense of humor; is creative; resists cultural conformity; and has a tendency toward self-growth.
The Fully-Functioning Person	Carl R. Rogers (1951)	The **fully-functioning person** makes increasing use of his/her organism and all available information; is free to choose behaviors and experiences that are genuinely satisfying; is able to trust his/her organism and to experience feelings fully; is highly open to evidence from all sources; and is completely engaged in the process of being and becoming.
The Effective Person	Donald Blocher (1974)	The **effective person** is consistent in behavior and committed to goals and purposes; is able to control emotional impulses and responses (particularly frustration, ambiguity, and hostility); is competent in coping with environment; and exhibits creativity in thoughts and actions.

Table 2 (continued)

Models of Mental Health as General Goals for Counseling

Models of Mental Health	Authors of Models	Descriptions of Models
The Mature Person	Gordon Allport (1961)	The **mature person** extends the concept of self to others; can relate warmly to others in both intimate and superficial ways; possesses emotional security and accepts self; perceives, thinks, and acts with enthusiasm in accord with reality; has self-insight and self-understanding; and lives in harmony with a unifying philosophy of life.
The Adequate Person	A. Combs & D. Snygg (1959)	The **adequate person** perceives self in positive ways; is capable of accepting and integrating his/her perceptions in the phenomenal field; has a broad identification of self with others; and is likely to be an agent of social change rather than one resigned to the status quo.
The Normal Person	C.J. Shoben (1957)	The **normal person** has self-control; is integratively adjusted; possesses a sense of personal and social responsibility; has a "democratic social interest and a commitment to ideals and standards"; shows a tendency toward the fulfillment of his/her human potentialities; and does not define self in relationship to statistical norms.

definitions (Ryckman, 1985).

- A theory (a) is a set of stated postulates or assumptions, (b) has a set of related concepts with definitions, and (c) functions to predict new facts or relations and to integrate what is already known (Patterson, 1986).

- A theory is a set of statements consisting of propositions which explain factual data derived from observation and/or experimentation (Wolman, 1973).

- A theory is a systematic conceptualization of interrelated propositions for the purpose of defining a problem or explaining and predicting phenomena (authors' definition).

The Functions of Theory (What It Does)

1. Serves as a framework for practice (e.g., the practice of counseling).
2. Stimulates research studies.
3. Serves as a framework for prediction and explanation of phenomena.
4. Serves as a framework for existing facts and observations.
5. Provides clarity in the case of complex problems and phenomena.

The Criteria of a Good Theory

1. IMPORTANCE　(applicability, relevance, and degree of acceptance)
2. CLEARLY STATED AND PRECISE　(well-written and understandable)
3. PARSIMONY AND SIMPLICITY　(economically stated, not too many concepts, and simply stated)
4. COMPREHENSIVENESS　(accounts for a wide range of phenomena)
5. TESTABLE AND OPERATIONAL　(convertible to measurement, operational terms, and research testing of propositions)
6. EMPIRICAL VALIDITY　(supported by research studies and literature and capable of valid predictions)
7. HEURISTIC/STIMULATING　(stimulates interest, provokes thought and further development, stimulates research)
8. APPLIED VALUE　(has value for solutions to human problems)

References

Hall, C.S., & Lindzey, G. (1978). Theories of personality (3rd ed.). New York: John
    Wiley.

Patterson, C.H. (1986). Theories of counseling and psychotherapy (4th ed.). New York:
    Harper & Row.

Ryckman, R.M. (1985). Theories of personality (3rd ed.). Monterey, CA: Brooks/Cole:

Wolman, B.B. (Ed.). (1973). Dictionary of behavioral science. New York: Van Nostrand
    Reinhold.

Notes

SECTION 2

Counseling Theories

005	ACTUALIZING THERAPY

Founder(s)/Proponents

Everett L. Shostrom

Lawrence M. Brammer

Assumptions

1. Each person is unique, however, shares commonalities with other human beings.
2. Among the time modalities, the "present" or "here-and-now" is the most important.
3. The person seeks self-fulfillment and possesses the freedom to choose.
4. The person is ultimately responsible for his or her actualizing or growth.
5. Behavior is primarily a learned phenomenon that is basically dependent upon the learning process.
6. The basic vehicle to actualizing is through social interaction with helping persons. (See Shostrom, 1976; Brammer & Shostrom, 1982.)

Concepts

Actualizing	Individual uniqueness	Freedom
Responsibility	Personal Orientation Inventory	Learning
Multidimensional	Developmental stages	Here-and-Now

Goals of Counseling

Self-Fulfillment	Interpersonal effectiveness	Awareness
Responsibility	Self-Actualization	Freedom
Spontaneity	Independence	Authenticity

Techniques of Counseling

    Reflection of feeling   (reexpression of client's feelings or attitudes)

    Reflection of experience   (reflection of nonverbal behavior of the client--
        both intended and unintended communication)

    Therapist's sharing of feelings   (therapist's sharing of own feelings)

    Intellectual interpretation technique   (interpretation of a variety of feelings)

    Body techniques   (activities and exercises for body awareness)

    Group techniques   (a variety of growth-group exercises)

Observations and Evaluation

1. Actualizing therapy borrows many ideas from other theoretical models (e.g., Maslow's self-actualization, learning theory, gestalt therapy, and client-centered therapy) and thus allows little room for new and original ideas of its own.

2. Although most goals of counseling are broad and difficult to define operationally, the theory does offer a means of measuring self-actualization (a primary goal of counseling) via use of the Personal Orientation Inventory (POI) and its subscales. Actualizing therapy also focuses on the value of evaluation of the counseling process and its outcomes.

3. There is a lack of discussion as to how the techniques and modalities of counseling can be applied to the counseling setting by problem of client and by nature of clientele population.

4. The theory is relatively comprehensive in accounting for a number of psychological concepts and principles that are related to counseling.

5. Although actualizing therapy calls itself a "therapy," it seems to be more of a theory of counseling since it focuses more on positive growth than on the correction of personality disorders.

References

Brammer, L.M., & Shostrom, E.L. (1982). Therapeutic psychology (4th ed.). Englewood Cliffs, NJ: Prentice-Hall.

Shostrom, E.L. (with L. Knapp & R. Knapp). (1976). Actualizing therapy: Foundations for a scientific ethic. San Diego: EdITS.

---

006   BEHAVIOR THERAPY
                          (Behavioral Counseling/Behavior Modification)

Proponents

Joseph Wolpe	Donald H. Meichenbaum
Julian Rotter	Jack Michael
John D. Krumboltz	Lee Meyerson
Carl E. Thoresen	Albert Bandura
John Dollard	Neal Miller

Assumptions

1. Most human behavior is learned (e.g., habits, neuroses, and phobias).
2. Learned behavior can be modified.
3. Human beings have drives and motives that propel them toward a goal. Some drives, such as fear and anxiety, are learned.
4. A cue or stimulus leads to a response. The strength of a response varies depending upon the intensity of a drive or a presenting stimulus.
5. Human beings, starting in early childhood, learn how to dispense stimuli in order to influence the behavior of others as well as conditions of their immediate environments.
6. Environmental cues or stimuli often determine time, place, and type of response evoked by the person.
7. A change in a person's environment can alter his or her behavior.
8. Positive reinforcement (or reward) of a behavioral response increases the probability of the reoccurrence or repetition of that response.
9. Withdrawal of a positive reinforcement results in a decrease in or cessation of a learned response--a phenomenon referred to as "extinction."
10. Learned responses can be transferred or generalized to new stimulus situations (e.g., fear of one situation being generalized to fear in a similar stimulus situation).
11. Therapeutic change is capable via learning mechanisms and models such as

classical conditioning, operant conditioning, social modeling, trial and error, and imagery.

Concepts

Learning	S-R (stimulus-response)	Chaining
Drive	Classical conditioning	Extinction
Cue	Operant conditioning	Generalization
Reinforcement	Schedules of reinforcement	Behavioral goals

Goals of Counseling

- Change in specific behavior
- Change in the frequency of a particular response
- Changes in behavior that are observable and measurable
- Correction of inappropriate behavior
- Resolution of phobias, anxiety, hysterical reactions, temper tantrums, sexual dysfunctions, unadaptive habits, and other specific behavioral disorders and problems.

Techniques of Counseling

Approval	Positive reinforcement	Social modeling
Fading	Systematic desensitization	Induced imagery
Shaping	Cognitive restructuring	Time out
Homework	Behavioral rehearsal	Role playing
Token economy	Assertiveness training	Behavior contract
Implosive therapy	Relaxation techniques	Emotional flooding
Aversive therapy	Self-Punishment	Reassurance

Observations and Evaluation

1. "Behavior therapy" is often used interchangeably or comparably with the concepts "behavioral therapy," "behavioral counseling" (Krumboltz' term), and "behavior modification."

2. Behavior therapy <u>claims</u> to be the most scientific and effective of the traditional theories of counseling and psychotherapy since its goals are specific (defined

in terms of the client's problem), observable, and measurable (Wolpe, 1981; Krumboltz, 1966).

3. Behavior therapy focuses on changing the client as well as the client's environment if necessary (i.e., stimulus conditions of the environment).

4. Behavior therapy has been accused of being manipulative (of the client) versus facilitative, and of treating the client as an object.

5. The questions of acceptable goals of counseling and appropriate reinforcement or stimulus for bringing about change are not clear in regards to the counseling process for particular client problems. Furthermore, the answers to these questions often depend too much upon the assumed ingenuity, sound judgment, creativity, and professional ethics of the counselor or behavior therapist.

6. Examples of applications of behavior therapy are presented in works by Krumboltz and Thoresen (1976) and Martin and Pear (1983). There are numerous theoretical models of behavior therapy, each emphasizing various focal points of learning theory or combining principles of learning with psychoanalytic concepts or other theoretical concepts. Table 3 presents summaries of four of the more popular theories of behavior therapy as examples of common themes as well as variations.

References

Krumboltz, J.D. (1966). Behavioral goals in counseling. Journal of Counseling Psychology, 13, 153-159.

Krumboltz, J.D., & Thoresen, C.E. (1976). Counseling methods. New York: Holt, Rinehart & Winston.

Martin, G., & Pear, J. (1983). Behavior modification: What it is and how to do it. Englewood Cliffs, NJ: Prentice-Hall.

Wolpe, J. (1981). Behavior therapy versus psychoanalysis. American Psychologist, 36, 159-164.

Table 3

Summaries of Four Theories of Behavior Therapy

Theories	Proponent(s)	Orientation	Terms or Concepts	Goals	Techniques
Reinforcement-Psychoanalytic Therapy	John Dollard and Neal Miller	Neurotic symptoms; combines psychoanalytic and learning principles; Hullian influence; views fear as learned	Drive, cue gradient, permissiveness, fear	Satisfaction of drives; lifting repression; insight; adaptive behavior	Labeling, imitation, reassurance, encouraging transference, free association, reward client's talking
Reciprocal Inhibition	Joseph Wolpe	Principles of classical and operant conditioning; use of extinction and training; all behavior is caused, thus client is not to blame	Reciprocal-inhibition, counterconditioning, anxiety, anxiety hierarchy	Eliminate neurotic symptoms or unadaptive behavior; "remove suffering"; improve human functioning	Clinical history; personality assessment; assertiveness training; desensitization (with relaxation); electric shock; drugs; induced imagery; emotional flooding; abreaction; aversive therapy; positive reinforcement; motivation
Social Learning Approach	Julian Rotter	Behavior is goal-directed; expectancy influences behavior; perceptions; person-environment interaction; role of language in behavior change	Construct, expectancy, language; reinforcement value; adjustive responses; generalization	Acquiring adjustive behavior; changing expectancies and reinforcement value; general self-improvement	Interpretation; verbal and direct reinforcement; structuring; reassurance; catharsis; suggestion
Behavioral Counseling	John Krumboltz	Useful with aggressive behavior, school learning problems; career counseling; focuses on decision making, altering maladaptive behavior, and preventing problems	Alternative solutions; behavioral statements; adaptive behavior	Observable and specific goals; individualized goals for each client; change of verbal behavior and operational behavior	Role playing; social modeling; verbal reinforcement

Note. From Dictionary of Counseling Techniques and Terms by F.D. Harper. Copyright 1981 by Douglass Publishers (Alexandria, Va.).

007   CLIENT-CENTERED THERAPY*

Founder/Major Proponent
    Carl R. Rogers

Assumptions

    The following is a summary of Rogers' (1951) 19 propositions or assumptions that underlie his theory of client-centered therapy.

1. Every person exists in a changing world of experiences of which he/she is the center.
2. The person (or the "organism") reacts to the environmental field as it is experienced and perceived, which is reality for that individual.
3. The person reacts as an organized whole to his/her environmental field.
4. The person's one basic tendency and striving is to actualize, maintain, and enhance the self.
5. Behavior is basically goal-oriented and represents one's attempt to satisfy needs.
6. Emotions accompany and facilitate goal-directed behavior; the intensity of an emotion is related to one's perceptions of the experience.
7. Behavior is best understood from the person's own internal frame of reference.
8. A part of one's total perceptual field gradually becomes differentiated as the self.
9. The self evolves from evaluational interactions of the person with the environment and with other human beings.
10. Values are attached to experiences and are a part of the self-structure (self-concept); they evolve from self-perceptions of experiences with others.

*Sometimes referred to as **person-centered therapy.**

11. Experiences are perceived in relationship to one's self-structure and are either symbolized, ignored, denied or distorted.

12. Ways in which one behaves are those which are often consistent with his or her concept of self.

13. Ways in which one behaves can also be inconsistent with the self; and thus such behavior is often denied by the person.

14. Maladjustment results from one's denial of experiences which are inconsistent with the self-structure.

15. Adjustment results from experiences of the organism that are consistent with the self-structure or concept of self.

16. Experiences that are inconsistent with the self-structure often lead to perceived threat and feeling of anxiety.

17. In the absence of threat (e.g., the counseling session), experiences that are inconsistent with the self can be examined, reorganized, and perceived in a more positive way.

18. As one perceives and accepts his/her own experiences, that person becomes more understanding and accepting of self and others.

19. As the individual perceives and accepts his/her experiences, that person gains new values that are more consistent with the self-structure.

Concepts

Self-Structure	Fully-Functioning person	Ideal self
Perception	Experiential field	Incongruence
Self-Regard	Unconditional positive regard	Congruence
Self	Empathic understanding	Organism
Values	Internal frame of reference	Reality

Goals of Counseling

Openness	Self-Direction	Less defensive
Congruence	Fully functioning	More realistic
Awareness	More objective perceptions	More accepting

Techniques of Counseling
- Reflection of content
- Reflection of feeling, attitude, or mood
- Reflection of core
- Acceptance (e.g., the comment, "um-huh")

Conditions of Effective Counseling

Client-Centered therapy emphasizes the importance of the interpersonal relationship between the counselor and the client. The following are conditions of the counselor-client relationship that Rogers (1951) cites as being necessary for effective counseling.

- The counselor's communication of <u>unconditional positive regard</u> (total acceptance of client's experience without conditions) toward the client.

- The <u>client's perception</u> of the counselor's communication of unconditional positive regard.

- The counselor's communication of <u>empathic understanding</u>; and the client's perception of the counselor's empathy.

- The counselor's necessary state of <u>congruence</u> vis-à-vis a client who is in a state of incongruence or disturbance.

Observations and Evaluation
1. Client-Centered therapy has been found to be very effective with persons who are incongruent, so-called neurotic, disturbed, or emotionally upset as well as those clients who tend to be highly verbal and introspective.

2. Client-Centered therapy has lacked effectiveness with clients who have crisis-oriented problems or multiple problems that require immediate action. These type problems are becoming increasingly more prevalent, especially in the large urban cities.

3. Many concepts of client-centered therapy are abstract and thus difficult to

operationalize for research study or translate into therapeutic practice (e.g., concepts such as empathy, congruence, unconditional positive regard, and reality).

4. The theory tends to ignore the use of assessment instruments (including psychological tests) and guidance information.

5. Client-Centered techniques (basically "reflection" and "acceptance") tend to be useful in the early stages of the counseling relationship for the purposes of establishing rapport and gaining understanding about the client's problem; however, they have decreased value for generating the client's action toward the resolution of a problem.

6. Client-Centered therapy is a passive approach (versus an action-oriented approach); it focuses on affective behavior (mainly feelings) versus cognitive behavior (thought, understanding, and judgment).

7. The client-centered therapist communicates genuineness and holds respect for each client as a human being of worth. Moreover, Rogers' theory posits that the nature of all human beings is primarily forward-moving, rational, realistic, and social.

8. Rogers' theory is one that emphasizes the tone and nature of the counseling process or "helping relationship" much more than it describes techniques of counseling (Rogers, 1958).

9. Client-Centered therapy is presented in unabridged form in Rogers' (1951) book by the same name. An excellent summary of the theory is outlined in Patterson's (1986) Theories of Counseling and Psychotherapy.

References

Patterson, C.H. (1986). Theories of counseling and psychotherapy (4th ed.). New York: Harper & Row.

Rogers, C.R. (1951). Client-Centered therapy. Boston: Houghton Mifflin.

Rogers, C.R. (1958). The characteristics of a helping relationship. Journal of Counseling & Development, 37, 6-16.

008   ECLECTIC COUNSELING

Founder/Proponents

Frederick C. Thorne (founder)   James O. Palmer

Lawrence M. Brammer   Robert Carkhuff & Bernard Berenson

Assumptions

The following summary is based on Thorne's (1968) 57 postulates from his theory of integrative psychology, which is the basis of his eclectic counseling approach:

1. The central attribute and need of the organism is that of integration (i.e., of experiences, conflicting tendencies, the sensory processes, organismic processes, psychological state, and integrates--or "integration of integrates").

2. Consciousness is the primary medium toward higher levels of integration. Consciousness is awareness of the unitized or total experience of the moment.

3. Self-Actualization results from higher levels of integration which results from improved psychological state.

4. Biological and social conditions (past and present) can influence development (in terms of limitations and probabilities); however, they are not necessarily direct causal factors.

5. The core of the personality is the self-concept which reflects both the personal and social expectations and which influences one's level of integration.

6. Behavior is primarily determined by environmental factors; however, the person is capable of self-control and thus free choice.

7. Psychopathology is mainly determined by biological and social factors that inhibit or limit higher levels of integration.

8. Behavior occurs in the form of integrated psychological states and complex behavior results from the integration of integrates.

9. Clinical diagnosis is the process of developing etiological equations that organize and explain psychological states.

10. Conditions of living and psychological states are capable of fluctuation and variance.

11. The basis of consciousness and higher levels of integration is awareness of self.

12. The organism in its conscious state is constantly sensing, perceiving, evaluating, and manipulating in relationship to past, present, and future factors.

Concepts

- Integration   (a process or state of higher organization of organismic functions and experiences that are brought together as a unified whole)

- Etiologic equations   (formal statements of causes related to behavior states and behavior disorders)

- Case handling   (a concept comparable to "counseling" or "psychotherapy" in meaning)

- Other concepts include self-concept, consciousness, perception, self-enhancement, psychological state, classification of personality disorders, and active versus passive techniques.

Goals of Counseling

- Self-Actualization

- Higher levels of organismic integration

- Improved psychological states of the organism or person

- Greater awareness of experiences of the moment

Techniques and Methods of Counseling

1. Diagnosis   (determining causation and implications of behavior)
2. Total push   (applying a number of treatment methods all together in a concentrated manner)
3. Masterful inactivity   (employing justification and explanation to delay or postpone a client's action (usually action that may result in harm to the client)
4. Tutoring (tutorial counseling)   (teaching the client to understand self and environment; also providing skills for coping)
5. Symptomatic therapy   (various techniques employed for the purpose of relieving symptoms--a necessary step for further treatment)

6. Passive listening (attentive and intensive listening in order to allow the client
        to vent hostility, anxiety, and other forms of resistance)
7. Developing an etiologic equation (creating verbal and algebraic equations that
        explain causation and psychological state for each client; e.g.,
        "low self-concept + lack of confidence = poor performance =
        inferiority complex")
8. Also appropriate techniques from other counseling theories; techniques that in-
    clude case history, reassurance, suggestion, silence, and encouragement.

Observations and Evaluation

1. Thorne's version of eclectic counseling is more systematic and rigorous as
   compared to those viewpoints of other proponents, who tend to offer a hodge-
   podge of techniques that appear to be appropriate for specific client problems.

2. Thorne's eclectic approach seems to be one of the most comprehensive theories
   of counseling, especially in terms of explaining human behavior and offering
   techniques and methods for treatment. However, the theory tends to neglect
   the affective aspects of human behavior.

3. It is not clear as to how the counselor arrives at the etiologic equations for the
   many different types of problems and clients or how quantitative weights or
   values are assigned to algebraic variables in the equation.

4. The comprehensiveness of Thorne's knowledge and the rigor of his thoughts come
   through in his many writings, and thus reflect his many years of formal training
   in both psychology and medicine.

5. Although eclectic theory is comprehensive, it lacks defined methods that are
   related to special populations, group processes, and a variety of counseling
   concerns. The focus of eclectic counseling tends to be toward individual counseling with persons who have personality disorders or psychopathologies.

6. Palmer's (1986) version of eclectic counseling is not as systematic as that of
   Thorne's; however, it is highly practical in offering a myriad of behavioral and
   dynamic techniques for defined problems, populations, and counseling settings.

7. Brammer (1988) and Carkhuff and Berenson (1977) discuss an "integrative approach" to the helping relationship (i.e., recommending appropriate techniques from different theories), which is eclectic by orientation; however, they tend not to classify themselves under the rubric of eclecticism.

8. Eclectic counseling in the original works of Thorne was set forth as a systematic and consistent theory. However, today it is often viewed loosely and popularly as a counseling approach that is flexible and broad in the application of techniques from different theoretical approaches with little regard for systematic diagnosis or orderly steps.

References

Brammer, L.M. (1988). The helping relationship: Process and skills (4th ed.). Englewood Cliffs, NJ: Prentice-Hall.

Carkhuff, R.R., & Berenson, B.G. (1977). Beyond counseling and therapy (2nd ed.). New York: Holt, Rineholt & Winston.

Palmer, J.O. (1986). A primer of eclectic psychotherapy. Monterey, CA: Brooks/Cole.

Thorne, F.C. (1968). Psychological case handling (Vol. 1). Brandon, VT: Clinical Psychology Publishing.

009   **EXISTENTIAL COUNSELING***

Proponents

Viktor Frankl	C. Gratton Kemp
Rollo May	Paul Tillich
Ludwig Binswanger	Jean Paul Sartre
Erich Fromm	Clemmont E. Vontress

Assumptions

1. The person is capable of and responsible for his or her actions.

2. The human being is capable of choosing, exercising freedom, and becoming.

3. The person has a capacity for awareness of self and surroundings of the moment.

---

*Sometimes referred to as **existential psychotherapy** and **existential therapy.**

4. The person has the ability to transcend or go beyond his/her immediate situation or the immediate present.

5. The essence of behavior is that of being (awareness of self) and becoming (striving toward growth and self-actualization).

6. The human organism functions as an integrated whole.

7. Human beings determine culture more than culture determines behavior or human destiny.

8. The major source of anxiety is a fear of losing others, of being alone.

9. Guilt results from one's inability to act.

10. The primary purpose of counseling is to help the person to act, accept responsibility for actions, and accept freedom to choose.

11. "Meaning in life" is a primary motivator of human existence and human functioning.

12. All human beings have a basic need to love and be loved, to feel a sense of relatedness to others.

Concepts

Being	Freedom of choice	Growth
Becoming	Freedom to act	Existence
Meaning	Transcendence	Guilt
Responsibility	Aloneness	Anxiety

Goals of Counseling

- Facilitating the client's self-understanding and self-growth.
- Improving the client's encounters with others.
- Expanding the client's world.
- Helping one to discover meaning for existence.

Counseling Techniques: An Outline & Overview

Techniques of Counseling

1. Understanding (use of skills, such as attentive listening, in order to acquire an existential understanding of the client's concerns; also communicating a sense of understanding of the client's behaviors and concerns)

2. Reflection of feeling (reflection of the client's feelings with a tone of personal warmth toward the client and understanding of the client's concerns)

3. Acceptance (acceptance of the client as a person of worth and acceptance of what the client is attempting to communicate)

4. Confrontation (nonthreatening confrontation aimed at getting the client to act)

5. Interpretation (to infer meaning related to the client's behavior as based on concepts of existentialism such as anxiety, guilt, aloneness, and love)

6. De-Reflection (in Frankl's logotherapy, a technique which helps the client to ignore anticipated anxiety by diverting his or her attention to something else)

7. Paradoxical intention (in Frankl's logotherapy, a technique of getting the client to confront anxiety and prepare for an anticipated anxiety-provoking situation)

Observations and Evaluation

1. Different viewpoints of existential counseling emphasize specific concepts of existentialism. For example, Viktor Frankl's logotherapy (a form of existential counseling) emphasizes meaning of life and spiritual aspects of life.

2. Some existential counseling viewpoints employ psychoanalytic techniques and concepts or serve as an adjunct approach to psychoanalysis.

3. Existential counseling is more of a theory of personal growth and prevention than one of counseling and psychotherapy. That is, since it focuses more on self-actualization, improved human functioning, and interpersonal effectiveness than on personality disorders or psychopathology.

4. The techniques and actual steps of existential counseling are not clearly defined.

The viewpoints of existential counseling seem too often to focus on the essence or tone of the counselor-client relationship rather than on the "how."

5. Outcomes of existential counseling are difficult to assess, evaluate, and observe; i.e., since goals are stated in general terms such as self-actualization, self-understanding, and meaning.

6. The flexibility of the counseling process and the counselor's positive and warm relationship toward the client may in themselves contribute to improved feeling and clarity for certain types of clients who may be confused, mildly emotionally upset, or lacking in a sense of direction in life.

7. Shertzer & Stone (1980), Downing (1975), and Carkhuff and Berenson (1977) provide overviews of various viewpoints of existential counseling, while Patterson (1986) presents an excellent review of Frankl's logotherapy version of existential counseling. Also see Frankl's (1984) Man's Search for Meaning: An Introduction to Logotherapy.

References

Carkhuff, R.R., & Berenson, B.G. (1977). Beyond counseling and therapy (2nd ed.). New York: Holt, Rineholt & Winston.

Downing, L.N. (1975). Counseling theories and techniques: Summarized and critiqued. Chicago: Nelson-Hall.

Frankl, V.E. (1984). Man's search for meaning: An introduction to logotherapy (3rd ed.). Boston: Beacon.

Patterson, C.H. (1986). Theories of counseling and psychotherapy (4th ed.). New York: Harper & Row.

Shertzer, B., & Stone, S.C. (1980). Fundamentals of counseling (3rd ed.). Boston: Houghton Mifflin.

010   **GESTALT THERAPY**

Founder/Major Proponent

Frederick "Fritz" Perls

Assumptions

1. The human being is a unified organism who functions as a whole and who
   is capable of feeling, thinking, and acting.

2. The basic tendency of the organism is a striving for balance (or homeostasis)
   through the process of self-regulation. Self-Regulation is achieved via
   the satisfaction of psychological and physiological needs.

3. Need satisfaction facilitates organismic balance and the completion of the
   Gestalt (whole pattern). Upon awareness of a need, the individual attempts
   to satisfy that need by either adjusting his or her behavior to the environment
   or adjusting the environment to his or her behavior.

4. The organism's primary inborn motives or goals are toward "self-preservation"
   and actualization of the self.

5. Aggression is the organism's expression toward attempting to satisfy a need
   or resisting satisfaction of a need.

6. Reality is what the organism selects to perceive from his or her environment,
   which is based on his or her changing needs and interests.

7. Anxiety represents the gap between the "now" and the "later"; it is tension
   that accompanies an anticipated event.

8. Psychological growth results from sensory awareness and through assimilation
   from environmental contact. Growth is thwarted or frustrated when the
   individual's contact with environment, in order to satisfy a need, is interrupted
   or rejected, thus closing opportunity for completion of the Gestalt.

9. The "now" is all that matters in therapy since the past only exists in present
   memory and the future only exists in present anticipation or expectation. Moreover, the past often exists in the present as unfinished business or as an incomplete picture that is in need of therapeutic closure.

10. The key to therapy is to get the person to re-own parts of the personality that are disowned due to their inconsistency with one's self-image; it involves restoring the wholeness of the individual and thus facilitating his or her growth.

11. Therapy should be concerned with the "what" of behavior (not the "why"), the here-and-now, and present behavior.

Concepts

Whole	Perceived pattern	Dreamwork
Awareness	Here-and-now	Integration
Needs	Relatedness of opposites	Responsibility
Growth	Nonverbal cues	Balance
Perception	Rules and games	Unfinished business

Other concepts include:

- Topdog (a part of the personality structure that represents "shoulds" and "should nots"; similar to Freud's superego)
- Underdog (representation of primitive urges; parallel to Freud's id)
- Gestalt (whole, perceived pattern, configuration, or summary of integrated parts)
- Contact boundary (point of contact between the person and the environment)
- Confluence (state of behavior in which one does not perceive boundaries between self and environment; also behavior where one has difficulty in tolerating differences in others)
- Hunger instinct (an instinct or drive toward self-preservation of the individual organism)

Goals of Counseling

- Growth or actualization of the self
- Organismic balance, optimal functioning, improved sensory awareness
- A re-owning of disowned parts of the personality
- Organismic self-regulation
- Resolution of unfinished business (e.g., unresolved past experiences)

Techniques and Methods of Counseling

1. Empty chair (client role plays with an imaginal person who is represented in an empty chair)

2. Hot seat (group leader focuses on one member of the group at a time with intermittent input from other members)

3. Concentration (process of getting the client to focus on the necessary concern of the moment in order to complete unfinished business or the Gestalt pattern)

4. Shuttle technique (method of shifting the client's attention back and forth between two topics or activities in order to facilitate awareness)

5. Dreamwork (client relives a dream through talking and/or acting out all parts and characters in the dream)

6. Monotherapy (client creates and writes a dramatic scene and role plays personal fantasies and repressed wishes in order to facilitate awareness)

7. Homework (activities assigned for the client to carry out between sessions)

8. Role reversal (client is requested to role play a role of another person or one that is opposite to that of his or her natural behavior)

9. Confrontation (nonthreatening confrontation of resistance and disowned behavior)

10. Sharing hunches (group members' sharing of feelings and perceptions of other members in a tentative manner or in the form of "hunches")

11. Closure (process of facilitating the client's completion of an unfinished experience, feeling, or thought; or completion of the "whole picture" or unfinished business)

12. Rules and games (techniques and exercises used in groups such as "making the rounds," "I take responsibility," and "I have a secret")

Observations and Evaluation

1. According to Perls, Gestalt therapy was influenced by Gestalt psychology, psychoanalysis, and the Eastern thoughts of Buddhism and Taoism.

2. Although the theory is applicable to individual counseling, many of its techniques and methods appear to be more relevant to the group therapy setting.

Gestalt therapy has made numerous contributions to group work in terms of its many innovative group techniques and exercises. However, the authoritarian group leadership on the part of the Gestalt therapist and the structuring of group activities allow little freedom for the group members.

3. The use of Gestalt therapy in individual counseling or the one-to-one counseling relationship is not clearly described in terms of steps and techniques of counseling.

4. The Gestalt therapist takes much leadership and responsibility for therapeutic activity and change; therefore, the effectiveness of the theory appears to depend a lot on the personality, style, technical skills, and charisma of the therapist.

5. There is limited research that documents the effectiveness and successes of Gestalt therapy as a theoretical approach. The popularity of the therapy seems to have been influenced more by "Fritz" Perls the man, Perls' many demonstrations of the therapy (both in public and on film), and by the attractiveness of its role-playing techniques, exercises, and games.

6. Along with concepts of Gestalt psychology, psychoanalysis, and Eastern religions, Gestalt therapy also reflects concepts and principles of existentialism and perceptual-phenomenology. Gestalt therapy is so comprehensive in background and application of techniques/methods that it may even be viewed as an eclectic approach.

7. For a general discussion of Gestalt therapy see Perls (1969). In regards to the applications of Gestalt therapy techniques in the group setting, refer to Hansen, Warner, and Smith (1980). Moreover, Corey (1986) and Patterson (1986) present chapter summaries of Gestalt therapy.

References

Corey, G. (1986). Theory and practice of counseling and psychotherapy (3rd ed.). Monterey, CA: Brooks/Cole.

Hansen, J.C., Warner, R.W., & Smith, E.J. (1980). Group counseling: Theory and process (2nd ed.). Chicago: Rand McNally.

Patterson, C.H. (1986). Theories of counseling and psychotherapy (4th ed.). New York: Harper & Row.

Perls, F.S. (1969). Gestalt therapy verbatim. Lafayette, CA: Real People Press.

011   **PSYCHOANALYSIS**

Founder/Major Proponent*

Sigmund Freud

Assumptions

1. Behavior is determined by intrapsychic factors such as biological impulses and instinctual drives.

2. The human organism is irrational and animalistic with a drive toward self-gratification, basically sexual gratification.

3. Practically all behavior is meaningful (not accidental) and is often expressed in symbolism. Behavioral or psychic events tend to be preceded by other psychic events.

4. The structure of personality is divided into three parts or components: the **id** (instinctual and biological urges that seek immediate gratification); the **ego** (mediator of acceptable expression of id impulses based on societal realities); and **superego** (the conscience and the ego-ideal based on parental morals and values).

5. The personality or the psychic mind is partly conscious and partly unconscious. It actually consists of the **conscious** (thoughts/feelings of which one is aware), the **preconscious** (things that can be recalled to awareness), and the **unconscious** (things that have been forgotten and cannot normally be recalled).

6. Development is psychosexual and includes the following stages which are associated with pleasure and energy centered around a particular area of the body during a given age period: **oral stage** (satisfaction centered around stimulation

---

*See page 37 for neo-Freudian proponents such as Adler, Fromm, Horney, and Jung.

of the mouth--infancy to age 1);   **anal stage** (satisfaction from eliminating or withholding feces--ages 2 to 3);   **phallic stage** (focus on energy of the genitals and on one's sexual identity--ages 4 to 5);   **latency period** (lack of sexual interest and expression--age 6 to puberty); and **genital stage** (period of sexual tension and activities--adolescence through adulthood).

7. Behavior disorders, requiring therapy, result from conflict involving components of the personality (id, ego, and superego), fixations at a particular psychosexual stage, or excessive use of defense mechanisms.

8. Anxiety results from intrapsychic conflict among the id, ego, and superego (or between any two of these) as well as from external realities of one's surroundings.

9. Parental beliefs and past experiences are significant influencers on the presenting behavioral characteristics and symptoms of the client or patient.

10. The primary focus of therapy or counseling should be the resolution of intrapsychic conflict and the facilitation of insight.

Concepts

Id	Psychosexual development	Dreams
Ego	Personality structure	Instincts
Superego	Personality dynamics	Drives
Conscious	Oedipal complex	Conflict
Preconscious	Pleasure principle	Anxiety
Unconscious	Reality principle	Sex
Determinism	Past experiences	Cathexis

Other concepts include:

- Fixation   (a phenomenon characterized by a "clinging" to behavioral patterns associated with a particular stage of psychosexual development)
- Transference   (the client's expression of feelings and attitudes toward the counselor in a way that he or she has related to a significant person in the past)

- Countertransference (the counselor or therapist's expression of feelings and attitudes toward the client in a manner in which he or she has related to a significant person of the past)
- Material (therapeutic information and symbolism shared by the client during the psychoanalytic process)
- Libido (the basic source of energy that is housed in the id and which drives the organism to take action; it consists primarily of sexual impulses)
- Defense mechanisms (unconscious methods employed by the person as a means of dealing with anxiety and pressures imposed by the id and superego; e.g., repression, rationalization, projection, and denial)
- Psychoanalysis (a theory of personality as well as a theory of psychotherapy that emphasizes biological impulses and unconscious motives)

Goals of Counseling

- Facilitating insight
- Resolving intrapsychic conflict
- Minimizing resistance and defensiveness
- Reducing anxiety

Techniques of Counseling (Psychoanalysis)

1. Interpretation (counselor's inferring of meaning and causes of the client's behavior based on symbolic material (including symbols in dreams), past experiences, and unconscious motives)
2. Free association (facilitating the client's open and uninhibited discussion of anything that comes to mind; the client sometimes lies on a couch in a relaxed state)
3. Catharsis (a talking out experience by the client in order to release tension or repressed feelings)
4. Abreaction (a cathartic technique employed in the early stage of therapy for the purpose of freeing psychic energy and facilitating the client's ability to discuss painful experiences)
5. Exploration (encouraging the client's discussion or exploration of past experiences and/or childhood experiences)

6. Dream analysis (interpretation of material and symbolism from dreams, often with meaning related to unconscious and sexual motives)

7. Transference analysis (interpretation of the client's transference behavior in facilitating his or her insight into the dynamics of past relationships)

8. Working through (a technique in the latter phases of psychoanalysis for the purpose of encouraging the client's expression of in-depth feelings, understanding of transference behavior, association of past experiences with present behavior, resolution of intrapsychic conflict, and/or movement toward insight)

Observations and Evaluation

1. Although classical psychoanalysis (as outlined above) is associated with the pioneering works of Sigmund Freud, there are neo-Freudians who have modified Freud's theory by deemphasizing instinctual and unconscious factors and emphasizing social, interpersonal, and individual-difference factors. The following is a list of popular neo-Freudians with their theoretical emphases and their variations from Freud's viewpoint:

Alfred Adler (inferiority versus superiority, power, lifestyle)

J. Dollard & N. Miller (psychoanalytic concepts in combination with learning theory concepts)

Erich Fromm (social influences, productiveness, love, identity)

Karen Horney (social determinants, human relationships, need for security)

Carl Jung (individuality, striving, personality types, introvert versus extrovert)

Otto Rank (dependency versus independence, birth trauma as roots of anxiety and conflict)

Harry Stack Sullivan (personality as the product of interpersonal relationships, pursuit of security)

2. Psychoanalytic theory is both a theory of personality and a theory of counseling and psychotherapy. Psychoanalysis, itself, represents the therapeutic process based on Freud's theoretical assumptions about human personality.

3. The etiology of the psychoanalytic viewpoint is based on Freud's clinical experiences and observations in regards to individual psychotherapy with his patients.

4. Freud's theory seems to overemphasize biological determinants, parental influences, motivation, symbolism in human behavior, and possibly the importance of unconscious factors.

5. The theory neglects environmental determinants of human behavior and the early influence of real and vicarious role models other than parents.

6. Freud's psychoanalytic theory was the first comprehensive theory of personality and psychotherapy dating back to the 1800's; and, therefore, has contributed much to the field of psychology. Its modern following is especially evident among psychiatrists and clinical psychologists.

7. Psychoanalysis is a long-term therapy that is appropriate with cases of intra-psychic conflict. It has had little value in terms of crisis problems and problems that are highly prevalent among low-income groups and/or American racial minorities.

8. The process of psychoanalysis has been criticized as being difficult to research or evaluate (Ryckman, 1985) and as having low rates of documented success (Wolpe, 1981); however, the approach continues to enjoy much popularity and respect.

9. For background readings on psychoanalysis, see The Life and Work of Sigmund Freud (Jones, 1961) or A Primer of Freudian Psychology (Hall, 1979); the latter is a brief summary of Freud's work. For explanations and case examples of the applications of psychoanalysis (including neo-Freudian approaches), see Morse and Watson (1977), Watson (1978), Weiner (1983), and Bernstein and Nietzel (1980).

References

Bernstein, D.A. & Nietzel, M.T. (1980). Introduction to clinical psychology. New York: McGraw-Hill.

Hall, C.S. (1979). A primer of Freudian psychology (25th ed.). New York: The New American Library.

Jones, E. (edited and abridged into one volume by L. Trilling & S. Marcus). (1961). The life and works of Sigmund Freud. New York: Doubleday.

Morse, S.J., & Watson, R.I., Jr. (Eds.). (1977). Psychotherapies: A comparative casebook. New York: Holt, Rinehart & Winston.

Ryckman, R.M. (1985). Theories of personality (3rd ed.). Monterey, CA: Brooks/Cole.

Watson, R.I. (1978). The great psychologists: From Aristotle to Freud (4th ed.). New York: J.B. Lippincott.

Weiner, I.B. (Ed.). (1983). Clinical methods in psychology (2nd ed.). New York: John Wiley.

Wolpe, J. (1981). Behavior therapy versus psychoanalysis: Therapeutic and social implications. American Psychologist, 36, 159-164.

012   RATIONAL-EMOTIVE THERAPY

Founder/Major Proponent

Albert Ellis

Assumptions

1. The human organism is rational as well as irrational.

2. Neurosis is the result of irrational and illogical thinking.

3. Unhappiness is caused by irrational thoughts and irrational self-verbalizations. Irrational thoughts result from beliefs, attitudes, and perceptions.

4. Parental teachings and early experiences in development influence beliefs and attitudes which in turn influence irrational thinking.

5. Emotional disturbance and neurosis are accompanied by irrational thoughts and irrational self-verbalizations.

6. Emotion accompanies thinking; therefore, emotions and thoughts are not mutually exclusive. Moreover, thoughts are often biased, prejudiced, and irrational.

7. Irrational thinking and thus emotional disturbance are maintained by one's self-verbalizations of illogical beliefs and perceptions.

8. Behavior does not result from a presenting stimulus but from one's perception of the stimulus (represented by Ellis' "A-B-C Theory").

Concepts

- Self-Verbalizations (irrational statements that the client tells himself or herself which serve to maintain irrational behavior and thus emotional disturbance)
- Irrational thinking (thinking that has no logical bases, illogical thoughts, biased thinking that is accompanied by emotion)
- Re-Think (refers to the process of getting the client to change from illogical or irrational thinking to rational thinking)
- Re-Verbalization (refers to getting the client to verbalize his or her concerns in logical expressions as opposed to illogical verbalizations)
- A-B-C Theory (actually, a principle which posits that one's belief ["B"] about an activating event ["A"] causes a given behavioral consequence ["C"] and not the event itself)*
- Rational living (refers to a whole lifestyle and philosophy of living rationally)
- Other concepts (other theoretical concepts include beliefs, perceptions, attitudes, rational thinking, irrational ideas, and happiness versus unhappiness)

Goals of Counseling

- Rational thinking
- Rational living
- Happiness
- Responsibility
- Self-Actualization
- Elimination of anxiety, depression, and feeling of inferiority

---

*Also see Ellis' A-B-C-D-E version of this principle. The "D" represents "a disputing of irrational beliefs" and the "E" represents the "effect of disputing" or the new rational behavior that results.

Techniques of Counseling

1. Rapport-Gaining technique (facilitating free expression from the client and helping the client to relax—especially during the beginning of the counseling relationship)

2. Teaching (providing information, understanding, and reeducation in regards to illogical beliefs; teaching the client to re-think and re-verbalize irrational expressions)

3. Attacking (verbally attacking irrational thoughts and ideas)

4. Persuasion (persuading the client to alter irrational beliefs and attitudes)

5. Suggestion (suggesting alternative ways of perceiving self and the world, i.e., in more rational ways)

6. Prescription of activities (prescribing new behaviors as well as assignments that facilitate rational living)

7. Encouragement (providing support for the client's attempts toward rational behavior and rational living)

Steps of Counseling

Step 1: Show the client that he/she is illogical or irrational.

Step 2: Relate the client's irrational thoughts to his/her problem and unhappiness.

Step 3: Get the client to change his/her thinking; to get rid of irrational ideas.

Step 4: Develop in the client a whole rational philosophy of living.

Observations and Evaluation

1. In the classic work describing his theory, Ellis (1984) presents "eleven irrational ideas" of human nature that have become popular among counselors.

2. In terms of critical evaluation, Patterson (1986) notes that rational-emotive therapy can be (a) ineffective with persons who are incapable of rational thinking (e.g., the mentally deficient, the severly disturbed, and the very young child) and (b) threatening to some clients in terms of its directive and confrontive techniques.

3. Rational-Emotive therapy seems to be especially effective with a wide variety of problems and personalities including crisis problems, multiple problems, and clients who tend to be irrational, highly anxious, phobic, and procrastinating.

4. For further reading on rational-emotive therapy, see the numerous works by Ellis and his associates (e.g., Ellis & Grieger, 1977; Ellis & Harper, 1975; and Maultsby & Ellis, 1974).

References

Ellis, A. (1984). Reason and emotion in psychotherapy. New York: Citadel Press. (Published originally by Lyle Stuart, 1962.)

Ellis, A., & Grieger, R. (Eds.). (1977). Handbook of rational-emotive therapy. New York: Springer.

Ellis, A., & Harper, R.A. (1975). A new guide to rational living (rev. ed.). Englewood Cliffs, NJ: Prentice-Hall. (Also published by Wilshire Books of Hollywood, CA.)

Maultsby, M.C., & Ellis, A. (1974). Techniques for using rational-emotive imagery (REI). New York: Institute for Rational Living.

Patterson, C.H. (1986). Theories of counseling and psychotherapy (4th ed.). New York: Harper & Row.

---

013   **REALITY THERAPY**

Founder/Major Proponent

William Glasser

Assumptions

1. The problems of human beings derive from their inability to fulfill essential needs.

2. Among the essential human needs expressed by persons in psychotherapy, the two most important are the need to love and be loved and the need to feel worthwhile to self and others.

3. Human beings often deny the world around them and break rules of society as they attempt to satisfy their needs in unrealistic and unacceptable ways.

4. All human beings have the same basic needs, but differ in their abilities to meet their needs.

5. The primary concern of psychotherapy is to help the client to meet his or her needs in responsible and realistic ways or within the context of a real world.

6. Responsible behavior is an expression of one's ability to meet his/her needs without depriving others of the ability to fulfill their needs.

7. The responsible person is also one who does things that bring a feeling of self-worth and a feeling of worth to others.

8. What is often labeled as mental illness is actually irresponsible behavior (except in the case of biologically based disorders). By the same token, mental health is synonymous with responsible behavior.

9. Responsibility and irresponsibility are learned behaviors that can be taught.

10. Human beings tend to acquire either a "success identity" or a "failure identity."

Concepts

Responsibility	Present behavior	Needs
Irresponsibility	Self-Worth	Love
What versus why	Reality	Identity

Goals of Counseling

- Responsible behavior
- Positive feelings of self-worth and worth to others
- Fulfillment of needs
- Acquisition of an identity of success

Techniques of Counseling (Therapy)

1. Teaching (special teaching or training in order to help the client to meet his/her needs in realistic and responsible ways)

2. Involvement (the counselor's communication with the client which is characterized by structure, commitment, emotional concern, mental toughness, openness, friendliness, and attentiveness)

3. Contract (agreement on responsible behaviors or assignments that the client must complete between counseling sessions; sometimes the contract is based on a handshake, verbal agreement, or written agreement between the client and the counselor)

4. No Excuses (counselor avoids entertaining or accepting excuses that most often represent and help to maintain irresponsible behavior; counselor sometimes simply ignores expressed excuses)

5. <u>Homework</u>   (assignment and prescription of activities designed to help the client fulfill needs and acquire responsible behaviors)

6. <u>Other Counseling Techniques</u> (commonly used techniques include confrontation, persuasion, role playing, humor, and modeling)

Steps of Counseling ("Procedures")

Step 1: <u>Become involved</u> with the client through active, intense, concerned, and open approach (maintain this tone throughout the counseling relationship).

Step 2: <u>Reject behavior that is irresponsible and unrealistic</u> while accepting the client as a person.

Step 3: <u>Teach the client to fulfill his/her needs in responsible and realistic ways.</u>

Rules and Characteristics of the Counseling Relationship

- The counselor focuses on <u>present behavior</u> and avoids delving into the past or the unconscious. The counselor is concerned about the "what" of behavior and not the "why."

- The counselor helps the client to make <u>value judgments</u> about his or her behavior; i.e., whether the behavior is responsible or irresponsible--realistic or unrealistic.

- The counselor <u>ignores the client's excuses</u> for unfulfilled commitments.

- The counselor helps the client to develop a <u>plan of action</u> toward accomplishing realistic goals.

- The counselor <u>solicits an expression of commitment</u> (to responsible action) from the client via some form of agreement or contract.

- The counselor <u>does not use punishment or threat</u> to evoke responsible action.

Observations and Evaluation

1. Reality therapy has been especially effective with difficult clients, including delinquent youth, culturally disadvantaged clients, alcoholics, and problem school youth.

2. Wubbolding (1975) warns that neophyte reality therapists often make several mistakes in counseling which can include (a) establishing insufficient involvement, (b) making the plan of action too vague or too general, (c) rushing or forcing results from the plan of action, and (d) proceeding too quickly to solicit commitment from the client.

3. Reality therapy gives little to no attention to past experiences, unconscious motives, and feelings of the client.

4. The counselor or reality therapist has to be cautious in imposing cultural-laden values and judgments related to what is responsible versus irresponsible and what is realistic versus unrealistic.

5. The theory puts a large amount of stock into individual responsibility and effort with little attention on how to deal with societal influencers, obstacles, and impasses that can preempt need-fulfillment and higher levels of success.

6. For background reading on reality therapy, see Corey (1986), Glasser (1965, 1984), and Wubbolding (1975).

References

Corey, G. (1986). Theory and practice of counseling and psychotherapy (3rd ed.). Monterey, CA: Brooks/Cole. (See Chapter 10, "Reality Therapy," p. 242.)

Glasser, W. (1965). Reality therapy. New York: Harper & Row.

Glasser, W. (1984). Reality therapy. In R. Corsini (Ed.), Current psychotherapies (3rd ed.). Itasca, IL: F.E. Peacock.

Wubbolding, R.E. (1975). Practicing reality therapy. Journal of Counseling & Development, 54, 164-165.

014   SYSTEMATIC COUNSELING

Proponents

Norman R. Stewart & Associates
Joseph H. Brown & Carolyn S. Brown

Assumptions

1. An effective model of counseling should be practical for application and should provide prescriptions of what should be done in the counseling process.

2. A counseling model or system should be a step-by-step guide or blueprint used by the counselor to identify the different functions and stages of counseling.

3. A blueprint for each client should show the movement of the client through the system as counseling progresses; checkpoints and destinations, the specific flow of information, and actions or decisions that occur throughout the counseling process.

4. The basic components of a counseling theory or model should be (a) a counselor, (b) a client, (c) a counseling system, and (d) outcomes of the counseling system.

5. The input into a system by both the client and the counselor determines the outcomes of that system.

Concepts

Flow-Chart	Blueprint	Outcomes
Prescriptions	Decision-Making	Referral
Learning	Information processing	Input
Error	Behavior contract	Stages

Other concepts include:

- System   (an organized assembly of interrelated components designed to function as a whole to achieve predetermined objectives)
- Feedback   (signals that suggest a need to redesign functions or behaviors performed by the client or counselor in order to correct or prevent mistakes in the counseling process)
- Recycling   (the repetition of counseling functions in order to correct counseling errors)

Goals of Counseling

1. The overall purpose of counseling is to help persons to attain personal goals that result in positive changes in their life.

2. Goals are based on specific concerns and needs of the client.

3. Goals are formulated based on the client's input and readiness and the counselor's ability to effectively work with the client toward the fulfillment of the goal (here the counselor makes a decision of whether to refer the client to another source of help or whether to continue the counseling process).

4. Goals are reduced to measurable subgoals or learning objectives that can be evaluated in terms of ongoing performance and testable outcomes.

5. Examples of goals of systematic counseling are to "improve the client's self-esteem," "reduce a male client's anxiety on dates," "improve social skills," "talk to a specific person without losing one's temper," and "maintain a steady job."

6. For additional examples of goals (with their related learning objectives), see Stewart, Winborn, Burks, Johnson, and Engelkes (1978) and Brown and Brown (1977).

Steps of Counseling

The number and sequence of steps can differ according to the goal and objectives for each client.

Step 1: Receive referral and evaluate appropriateness of referral.

Step 2: Explain counseling relationship and prepare for interview.

Step 3: Construct a model of client's concerns.

Step 4: Decide goal and objectives.

Step 5: Implement strategy.

Step 6: Evaluate client's performance.

Step 7: Terminate counseling.

Step 8: Monitor client's performance and evaluate counselor's performance.

Techniques of Counseling

Questioning	Information giving	Restatement
Referral	Verbal reinforcement	Interpretation

Other techniques include:

1. Maintaining tension in the interview (the use of silence, challenge, and provocation to maintain client motivation and involvement in the counseling process)

2. Managing pauses and silences (the counselor's use of patience during silent spots as well as skill in breaking silence that becomes nontherapeutic, i.e., by repeating key phrases of the client's last statement)

3. Recycling (a repetition of counseling functions in order to correct for errors)

4. Behavioral techniques (systematic counseling also employs various behavior therapy techniques such as time out, behavior contract, thought modification, modeling, rehearsal, and self-management)

Observations and Evaluation

1. Unlike most other counseling theories, systematic counseling provides a framework that maps the flow of the client through the system as well as the counseling process while also documenting counseling events and evaluating counseling performance and outcomes. Such a system assists in the maintenance of an accurate record of each client in counseling, plus it provides valid information for continuity between counseling sessions.

2. Systematic counseling allows for opportunities to detect and adjust for error via its feedback and recycling concepts. Types of errors include client error (faulty perceptions, irrational reasoning, and contradictory behavior), counselor error (resulting from failure of the counselor to control his/her behavior or failure to maintain consistency over sessions), and system error (faulty design in the system or instability of the system due to client or counselor error).

3. Systematic counseling seems to borrow numerous techniques from behavior therapy and directive counseling (trait-and-factor); however, has few innovative or original counseling techniques of its own. Moreover, the model provides little freedom for client decision-making and gives little or no attention to human feelings and individual differences.

4. The theory neglects discussion on the nature of human beings while focusing almost totally on systematic counseling as a model and process.

References

Brown, J.H., & Brown, C.S. (1977). Systematic counseling. Champaign, IL: Research Press.

Stewart, N.R., Winborn, B.B., Burks, H.M., Jr., Johnson, R.R., & Engelkes, J.R. (1978). Systematic counseling. Englewood Cliffs, N.J.: Prentice-Hall.

015   TRAIT-AND-FACTOR COUNSELING
(Also Called Directive Counseling or Minnesota Point of View)

Founders/Proponents

> Edmund G. Williamson
>
> Donald G. Paterson
>
> Frank Parsons

Assumptions

1. Human beings are born with the potential for good and evil; therefore, the purpose of counseling is to maximize the good and minimize the evil.

2. Human beings are rational (as opposed to irrational).

3. Development is not autonomous but requires the assistance and support of others.

4. The "good life" is to develop one's full potential, to self-actualize, to achieve excellence.

5. The goals of counseling and education are the same--to help students achieve their potentialities and to promote the optimum human development of the individual as a whole person (i.e., the intellectual, social, civic, and emotional development).

6. Counseling and psychotherapy are not the same; counseling is broader. Counseling deals with the rational or adjustment and psychotherapy deals with emotional problems.

7. Outcomes of counseling should be self-direction, self-understanding, social adjustment, and problem-solving ability.

8. Clients who come to counseling involuntarily or against their will can be helped,

although it is easier to help clients who volunteer.

Concepts

Self-Understanding	Problem-Solving	Prognosis
Decision-Making	Testing and appraisal	Diagnosis
Teaching	Social adjustment	Conformity

Goals of Counseling

- Development of the client's full potentialities
- Facilitation of the client's optimum development
- Self-Direction, self-understanding, social adjustment, and problem-solving ability

Steps of Counseling

Step 1: ANALYSIS (collecting all possible data related to the problem)

Step 2: SYNTHESIS (summarizing and organizing the data)

Step 3: DIAGNOSIS (counselor's conclusions about characteristics and causes related to the problem)

Step 4: PROGNOSIS (predictions of future developments based on the diagnosis)

Step 5: COUNSELING (actual steps or actions toward counseling goals)

Step 6: FOLLOW-UP (assisting the client with new or recurring problems and evaluating the effectiveness of the counseling action)

Techniques of Counseling

1. Advising (cautiously presenting advice, alternatives, and options to the client for consideration)

2. Persuasion (verbally influencing the strong consideration of a course of action)

3. Referral (transferring the client to a program or professional for further assistance)

4. Questioning (direct questions to the client concerning the problem, usually at the beginning of the interview more than at a later point)

5. Establishing rapport (efforts in the beginning of the counseling relationship aimed at establishing a natural, warm, and harmonious interaction with the client)

6. <u>Information giving</u> (sharing and sometimes interpreting information related to tests, occupations, training, and higher education)

Role of the Counselor

1. The counselor functions in the role of social model, teacher, and expert.

2. The counselor employs data-collecting instruments and procedures which include psychological tests, the interview, cumulative records, anecdotal records, and the autobiography.

3. The counselor helps the client to choose an appropriate environment, changes his or her present environment, and/or changes the client's attitudes.

Observations and Evaluation

1. Trait-and-Factor counseling was designed primarily for vocational and educational counseling; and, thus, has little application for personal-social counseling problems such as drug addiction, emotional problems, alcoholism, loneliness, and interpersonal conflict.

2. By counseling setting and population, trait-and-factor counseling has implications for school counseling, college counseling, and placement counseling--especially in regards to decision-making about educational and occupational choice.

3. Counselors are put in the role of resource person or "expert" when some clients of today (compared to when the theory was developed) may be just as sophisticated about themselves and the world.

4. Questions of validity can be raised in reference to multicultural use and interpretation of tests and other diagnostic tools, especially with America's racial minorities.

5. Observations by Patterson (1986) indicate that trait-and-factor theory (a) neglects the role of feelings in counseling, (b) puts too much confidence in diagnostic data, and (c) allows the counselor to play too large a role in influencing the decisions of the client.

6. For readings on trait-and-factor counseling or directive counseling, see Williamson (1950), Williamson (1972), and Chapter One in Patterson (1986).

References

Patterson, C.H. (1986). Theories of counseling and psychotherapy (4th ed.). New York: Harper & Row.

Williamson, E.G. (1950). Counseling adolescents. New York: McGraw-Hill.

Williamson, E.G. (1972). Trait-Factor theory and individual differences. In B. Stefflre & W.H. Grant (Eds.), Theories of counseling (2nd ed.). New York: McGraw-Hill.

016   **TRANSACTIONAL ANALYSIS**

Founder/Proponents

Eric L. Berne (founder)

Thomas A. Harris

Assumptions

1. All human beings have the need to contact others and to receive feedback and responses from others.

2. A transaction is the basic unit of social interaction between two persons. It is an exchange of strokes between two persons or the dispensing of a stimulus by one person and the reciprocal response by another person.

3. The structure of human personality consists of three components: the **parent** (internalized parental beliefs, values, and perceptions), the **adult** (the rational, realistic, and objective component that often regulates conflict between the parent and child), and the **child** (child-like, spontaneous, and creative component). (The three components are sometimes referred to as **PAC.**)

4. There are four basic positions which a person can hold in respect to perception of self and perception of others. They are:

   - **I'm not OK—you're OK**   (depressive or insecure position)
   - **I'm not OK—you're not OK** (psychotic or emotionally disturbed position)
   - **I'm OK—you're not OK**   (arrogant or better-than-thou position)
   - **I'm OK—you're OK**   (psychologically healthy position)

5. Human beings are not bound by past experiences and past transactions but rather they have the capacity to redecide, choose, and acquire alternative ways of relating to others.

6. Early parental teachings and expectations plus childhood decisions influence a person's life script or style of communicating with others.

7. The brain plays a key role in establishing human beings' relationships with each other in that it functions to (a) record, (b) recall, and (c) relive past experiences that reach back to early childhood.

8. Transactions between two persons can be analyzed in terms of the component of personality that sends the message and that component of another personality that responds to the message. Complementary transactions tend to be mutual, parallel, and healthy transactions between two reciprocating components of personality (e.g., adult-adult or adult-child) wherein crossed transactions tend to result in interpersonal conflict and communication breakdown due to uncomplementary transactions that usually involve three components of personality (e.g., the adult of one person sends a message to the adult of another person whose parent responds to the child of the initiating person).

9. There are many varieties of complementary and crossed transactions. They tend to occur in clusters or series which are employed to structure time for the purpose of interacting with other human beings. There are four ways of structuring time with others: (a) activities or formal procedures, (b) rituals, (c) pastimes, and (d) games.

10. Pastimes and games tend to be destructive and futile attempts to employ a sophisticated series of transactions for the immature fulfillment of one's need for intimacy.

Concepts

1. Transaction (the basic unit of social interaction; an exchange of strokes between two persons)

2. Complementary transaction (transactions that are mutual, parallel, and without conflict)

3. Crossed transaction (transactions that are in conflict and which lead to communication breakdown)

4. <u>Stimulus hunger</u> (the need for contact and response from others)

5. <u>Tactile hunger</u> (the need for physical closeness and intimacy)

6. <u>Recognition hunger</u> (the need for acknowledgement of existence by others)

7. <u>Structure hunger</u> (the need to organize and fill in time in order to avoid tension or boredom--often in reference to relating to others)

8. <u>Parent, adult, and child</u> (three forms of ego state or three components of personality structure--already defined under assumptions)

9. <u>Stroke</u> (the basic unit of a transaction; an exchange from one person to another)

10. <u>Script</u> (a complex set of transactions)

11. <u>Ritual</u> (socially prescribed behaviors in the form of complementary parental transactions--a way of structuring time)

12. <u>Games</u> (basically dishonest transactions that involve risk, payoff, and possible destruction)

13. <u>Pastimes</u> (complementary transactions that often fill in time or serve as small talk between persons with similar interests)

Goals of Counseling

- To resolve confusion
- To facilitate symptomatic control and relief as well as social control
- To provide readjustment and reorientation
- To help individuals to break away from ineffective scripts and thus live out the real selves in a real world
- To teach and facilitate more effective and rewarding social interactions

Techniques of Counseling

1. <u>Observation</u> (observing attentively for verbal and nonverbal signals of the client's behavior)

2. <u>Confrontation</u> (encountering inconsistencies in behavior)

3. <u>Explanation</u> (explaining a therapeutic point only when the "Adult" component of the personality is listening)

4. <u>Ego Gram</u> (using a diagram which explains the amount of time and energy that the client expends in each ego state--i.e., Parent, Adult, and Child)

5. <u>Karpman Triangle</u> (employing a triangle to represent and identify three primary game-playing roles of group therapy members--the roles of persecutor, rescuer, and victim)

6. <u>Specification</u> (reiterating a point that is therapeutically important to the client)

7. <u>Illustration</u> (using a light or humorous comparison or anecdote which serves as a follow-up to a confrontation)

8. <u>Interpretation</u> (interpreting meaning into distorted information that represents past experiences of the "Child")

9. <u>Crystallization</u> (communicating to the "Adult" of the client in the latter stages of counseling that it is OK to function <u>without</u> games or nonproductive transactions)

10. <u>Other Counseling Techniques</u> (other techniques employed--which need no special description--include questioning, teaching, and role playing)

Stages of Transactional Analysis

1. STRUCTURAL ANALYSIS: Identifies and describes the dynamics of the three ego states; also decontaminates the "Adult" from the "Child" and "Parent." (Therapy can be terminated here or the client can be continued in either psychoanalysis or transactional analysis.)

2. TRANSACTIONAL ANALYSIS: Teaches social control and healthy interaction with others.

3. ANALYSIS OF PASTIMES AND GAMES: Examines the client's transactions in pastimes and games and teaches the client the proper use and frequency of such transactions.

4. ANALYSIS OF SCRIPTS: Helps the client to transcend an ineffective life script and to develop a more constructive and productive script.

Observations and Evaluation

1. Transactional analysis has applications for problems related to interpersonal conflict and interpersonal effectiveness. Moreover, by setting, it is a theory that is very applicable to the group counseling or group therapy situation. In addition, transactional analysis has had implications for use with problems

related to human relations, social relations, employee relations, and alcoholism.

2. Harris (1969) describes the usefulness of transactional analysis with marital problems, children and adolescents, racial conflict, drug addiction, and other therapeutic concerns.

3. Corey (1986) states that although transactional analysis is useful and effective, it runs the risk of providing an intellectual experience for the client (via its numerous teachings and explanations) without provoking real-life behavior changes or the client's explorations of underlying feelings.

4. Patterson (1986) observes that transactional analysis is a complex theory but believed by many practitioners to be simple, is too closely similar to concepts and principles of psychoanalysis, and is burdened by a proliferation of terms with their special meanings.

5. For writings by the founder of transactional analysis, see Berne (1961, 1964, & 1972). Also note that on the popular scene of therapy, transactional analysis is simply referred to as "TA."

References

Berne, E. (1961). Transactional analysis in psychotherapy. New York: Grove.

Berne, E. (1964). Games people play. New York: Grove. (Also published by Ballantine, 1978.)

Berne, E. (1972). What do you say after you say hello? New York: Grove.

Corey, G. (1986). Theory and practice of counseling and psychotherapy (3rd ed.). Monterey, CA: Brooks/Cole. (See Chapter 7.)

Harris, T.A. (1969). I'm OK—You're OK. New York: Harper & Row.

Patterson, C.H. (1986). Theories of counseling & psychotherapy (4th ed.). New York: Harper & Row.

Notes

017   SUMMARY AND ANALYSIS OF THEORIES

Table 4 presents a summary of key concepts and characteristics of each theory, wherein Table 5 analyzes the orientation and foci of the theories based on several dimensions.

Table 4
Summary of Key Concepts and Characteristics of Theories

Theories/Proponents	Key Concepts	Key Techniques	Goals
Actualizing Therapy (Shostrom & Brammer)	Actualizing, responsibility, individual uniqueness, development	Reflection, Interpretation, body techniques	Self-Actualization, freedom, responsibility, interpersonal effectiveness
Behavior Therapy (Wolpe; Krumboltz; Dollard & Miller)	Learning, conditioning, reinforcement, drive, S-R, extinction	Reinforcement, modeling, approval, rehearsal, training techniques	Change in specific behavior; change in frequency/quality of a response
Client-Centered Therapy (Rogers)	Self-Structure, self, unconditional positive regard, perception, empathy, congruence vs. incongruence	Reflection of feeling and content, acceptance	Openness, congruence, self-direction, fully-functioning person
Eclectic Counseling (Thorne)	Case handling, etiologic equations, integration, consciousness	Tutoring, masterful inactivity, diagnosis, developing an etiologic equation	Self-Actualization, integration, greater awareness
Existential Counseling (Frankl; May; Fromm; Binswanger)	Being, becoming, meaning, freedom, responsibility, aloneness	Understanding, acceptance, interpretation	Self-Understanding, discovery of meaning, improved encounters

Table 4 (Continued)

Summary of Key Concepts and Characteristics of Theories

Theories/Proponents	Key Concepts	Key Techniques	Goals
Gestalt Therapy (Perls)	Whole, awareness, integration, here-and-now, gestalt, topdog, underdog	Empty chair, homework, dream-work, hot seat, confrontation, closure	Self-Regulation, organismic balance, actualization of the self
Psychoanalysis (Freud)	Id, ego, superego, unconscious, transference, dreams, psychosexual, drives	Interpretation, catharsis, free association, dream analysis, transference analysis	Insight, resolution of conflict, reduced anxiety
Rational-Emotive Therapy (Ellis)	Irrational thinking, self-verbalization, A-B-C Theory, re-verbalization, re-think	Teaching, persuasion, prescription of activities, encouragement	Rational thinking, rational living, happiness
Reality Therapy (Glasser)	Responsibility, reality, love, self-worth, needs, identity	Teaching, no excuses, contract, confrontation, homework, involvement	Responsible behavior, need-fulfillment, success identity
Systematic Counseling (Stewart, et al.; Brown & Brown)	Flow-Chart, error, feedback, input, decision-making, system, recycling, learning	Questioning, referral, information giving, verbal reinforcement, interpretation	Fulfillment of needs, achievement of personal objectives
Trait-and-Factor Counseling (Williamson)	Self-Understanding, decision-making, tests, adjustment, diagnosis, problem solving	Advising, teaching, referral, questioning, persuasion, information giving, gaining rapport	Self-development, self-understanding, problem-solving, decision-making

Table   4 (Continued)

Summary of Key Concepts and Characteristics of Theories

Theories/Proponents	Key Concepts	Key Techniques	Goals
Transactional Analysis (Berne; Harris)	Transaction, ego states (parent, child, adult), script, stroke, games	Observation, confrontation, explanation, ego gram, interpreta- tion	Effective interactions, improved script, resolved confusion

Notes

Table 5

Analysis of Theories by Focus and Orientation

Theories of Counseling	DIMENSIONS				
	Orientation of Goals — Insight(I) vs. Action(A)	View of Behavior — Determinism(D) vs. Free Will(FW)	Focus of Content — Cognitive(C) vs. Affective(A)	Type Counseling Model — Teacher-Learner(TL) vs. Self-Discovery(SD)	Nature of Process — Structured(S) vs. Unstructured(U)
Actualizing Therapy	I	FW	A	SD	U
Behavior Therapy	A	D	C	TL	S
Client-Centered Therapy	I	FW	A	SD	U
Eclectic Counseling	I	D	C	TL	S
Existential Counseling	I	FW	A	SD	U
Gestalt Therapy	I	D	A	SD	S
Psychoanalysis	I	D	A	SD	U
Rational-Emotive Therapy	A	D	C	TL	S
Reality Therapy	A	D	C	TL	S
Systematic Counseling	A	D	C	TL	S
Trait-and-Factor Counseling	A	D	C	TL	S
Transactional Analysis	I	FW	C	TL	S

(The poles of the dimensions above are not diametrically opposed or mutually exclusive in most cases. It is a decision of a theory being more focused or oriented toward one end of a dimension versus the other. For example, existential counseling and transactional analysis accept that much of behavior is determined, however, they view the person as having free will or choice. Moreover, although transactional analysis has been associated with semblances of affective theories such as psychoanalysis and Gestalt therapy, in its original form a la Berne, its concepts and techniques are oriented toward the cognitive side more than the affective.)

SECTION 3

Verbal Techniques

018   **REFLECTION**

Definition of Reflection

Reflection is a technique wherein the counselor mirrors what the client is feeling or saying during the moment (Rogers, 1951, 1961). Types of reflection include:

- Reflection of feeling (feeling or mood communicated by the client)
- Reflection of content (restatement or paraphrase of what the client says)
- Reflection of core (summarizing the essence or theme of a number of comments made by the client)

Purposes and Outcomes

1. Allows the counselor to be a sounding board or reflecting mirror whereby the client can receive feedback in the process of integrating disorganized or incongruent behavior and gain self-understanding.

2. Gives the client the responsibility for determining what is to be discussed in the counseling session.

3. Provides a free and nonthreatening atmosphere wherein the client can express behavior openly without fear of judgment or evaluation.

Applications of Reflection

1. Is the primary technique of client-centered therapy (Hokanson, 1983; Rogers, 1961).

2. Is effective with clients who come to counseling in an incongruent, unorganized,

or confused state; those who may have inner conflict or interpersonal conflict that needs resolving.

3. Is useful or effective with clients who are articulate, verbal, and introspective.

4. Can be employed in individual counseling, group counseling, group therapy, play therapy with children, and even classroom teaching.

5. Can be used to reflect both verbal and nonverbal behaviors of the client.

6. Is likely to be employed in school, college, and community settings with relatively normal clients who have personal-social problems or adjustment problems.

Role of the Counselor

1. Ohlsen (1974) notes that effective use of reflection by the counselor requires: (a) understanding the client, (b) developing a relationship in which the client feels safe, (c) recognizing when to respond, and (d) calling attention to the client's feelings without communicating his or her feelings as counselor.

2. According to Rogers (1951; 1961), the counselor can reflect the verbatim wording or paraphrase what the client has said. Moreover, the counselor's tone of voice, pauses, and emphasis on certain words and phrases are important in giving new and deeper meaning for the client's understanding—especially in a verbatim reflection.

3. Feelings, moods, and attitudes reflected by the counselor often include anxiety, shame, guilt, anger, excitement, dislike, boredom, affection, indifference, and love.

4. The counselor may introduce a reflection statement with phrases such as: "It seems like you..."; "There is sort of a feeling of..."; "What you are saying is..."; "I gather that you mean..."; "Let me play back what I hear you saying..."; or "There is this underlying feeling of...."

Examples of Reflection

Example 1: Reflection of Feeling
CLIENT: I've literally thrown my life away in gambling and drinking and now I have nothing to show for it.

COUNSELOR: I sort of sense that you have a feeling of regret and shame.

Example 2: Reflection of Content
CLIENT: The last year has been one big mess (pause)--just filled with turmoil and disappointments.

COUNSELOR: You seem to think things have just been very difficult and dis-appointing.

Example 3: Reflection of Core
CLIENT: I have talked about so many things; it's just getting even more confusing.

COUNSELOR: As I have heard you, the essence of what you've been saying for the last roughly 30 minutes is all concerning the question of whether or not to continue your college education here and the pressing need to go home to your husband and children whom you feel need you. You have also expressed a sense of loneliness and guilt, it seems, because of this temporary separation from your family.

Example 4: Use of Reflection in Play Therapy
CHILD: (A child three years of age enters the playroom and visually examines all the toys with a look of anticipation but indecision.)

COUNSELOR: There are many toys here (pause); it's hard to pick one.

CHILD: (Mounts a rocking horse and begins to rock with a reluctant smile.)

COUNSELOR: You like riding that rocking horse.

CHILD: Yeah, I want one--but Santa Claus didn't bring it.

Example 5: Use of Reflection in Group Counseling
GROUP MEMBERS: (Several members attack the leader for not giving active direc-tion or providing structure for the group's destiny and activity.)

GROUP LEADER: There is much anger here today aimed at me. It appears that some of you are holding me responsible for what we do in this group.

References

Hokanson, J.E. (1983). Introduction to the therapeutic process. Reading, MA: Addison-Wesley.

Ohlsen, M. (1974). Guidance services in the modern school. New York: Harcourt, Brace Jovanovich.

Rogers, C.R. (1951). Client-Centered therapy: Its current practice, implications, and theory. Boston: Houghton Mifflin.

Rogers, C.R. (1961). On becoming a person: A therapist's view of psychotherapy. Boston: Houghton Mifflin.

---

019   **INTERPRETATION**

Definitions of Interpretation

- An attempt by the counselor or psychotherapist to give meaning to or infer meaning from the client's behavior or past experiences.

- The counselor or psychotherapist's intervention aimed at unconscious material for the purpose of making the client aware of unconscious defenses, connections, wishes, and meanings (Morse & Watson, 1977).

Purposes and Outcomes

1. Connects unconscious material with conscious information which is already understood by the client.

2. Suggests reasons, explanations, purposes, and motivations for the client's actions in order to bring the client to a level of insight about his or her behavior.

3. Links causes (childhood influences, unconscious motives, and sexual motives) to behavior patterns and outcomes.

Applications of Interpretation

1. Is more frequently employed by psychoanalysts, psychiatrists, and traditional psychotherapists than by counselors.

2. Is applicable to psychoanalytic theory and existential psychotherapy in terms of use as a technique.

3. Is employed in the clinic, hospital, and private-therapy setting more than in the school-counseling setting.

4. Can be used with dream material (e.g., in dream analysis) in order to interpret unconscious desires, needs, and meanings.

Role of the Counselor/Psychotherapist

1. Interpretation is a technique that requires sophistication, cautious application, and timing. The counselor or psychotherapist should be sensitive to what to interpret, how deeply to interpret, and when to interpret.

2. The counselor should interpret carefully as the client reveals feelings and material from moment to moment or session to session. A premature or inaccurate interpretation can create client resistance.

3. Blocher (1974) suggests that the counselor should concentrate on "shallow" interpretations or interpretations that are already close to the client's level of consciousness or awareness.

4. Interpretations by the existential counselor (as opposed to those of the psychoanalyst) tend to focus on meanings related to existential concepts such as love, guilt, anxiety, and aloneness.

Examples of Interpretation

Example 1: Childhood Influences

CLIENT: I guess you think I have nothing good to say about my relationship with my mother, that is, since it seems that every time you mention her I respond somewhat critically and unpleasantly about my remembrances of her as a child.

COUNSELOR: One may also get the impression that you react similarly when you discuss your relationship with your wife.

Example 2: Sexual Theme

CLIENT: I always seem to be too busy to take up possible dates and opportunities for sex, you know? Like I've been seeing this girl, rather a classmate, after class at the rathskeller (pause); and we know that we want each other, but we

never talk about our feelings--only about sociological theories and class work.
It's like we just don't have enough time left to get into our feelings, you know?

COUNSELOR: It could be that intellectualizing is a safe way to avoid risks of the
unknown; like the risk of a new and different relationship, the possibility of being rejected if she does not reciprocate, and the anxiety of freeing up your
impulses and feelings. It's like, I guess, wanting to make a move but being
confronted by a lot of stop signs within your own mind.

Example 3: Alternative Interpretation

(This type interpretation provides an alternative interpretation to the one the
client makes; e.g., see Egan, 1986.)

CLIENT: I am disturbed by your receptionist's negative or, at least, indifferent
attitude toward me every time I come in to see you for counseling. She acts
like she is prejudiced toward Hispanics.

COUNSELOR: Have you considered that she may respond to others who come
here in a similar manner, regardless of ethnicity (pause); and that it may be
her own personality and not her reactions to you.

References

Blocher, D.H. (1974). Developmental counseling (2nd ed.). New York: Ronald Press.

Egan, G. (1986). The skilled helper: A systematic approach to effective helping (3rd
ed.). Monterey, CA: Brooks/Cole.

Morse, S.J., & Watson, R.I. (Eds.). (1977). Psychotherapies: A comparative casebook.
New York: Holt, Rinehart & Winston.

---

020   **ADVICE GIVING**

Definition of Advice Giving

Advice giving is a statement to the client that offers possible solutions, courses of
action, or recommendations in regards to a problem or concern (Ohlsen, 1974). Advice
giving is stronger than a mere suggestion. It goes beyond information giving in that it
involves the professional judgment, values, and opinions of the counselor.

Purposes and Outcomes

1. Stimulates action toward behavior change on the part of the client.

2. Provides the client with specific courses of action or defined options for consideration.

3. Offers a choice from three methods of advising: (a) **direct advice** (a frank statement or opinion), (b) **persuasive advice** (use of information or evidence to persuade the client), and (c) **explanatory advice** (explains diagnostic data and points out situations, alternatives, and implications). (See Williamson, 1950.)

Applications of Advice Giving

1. Is frequently employed as a technique in action-oriented counseling theories, especially trait-and-factor or directive counseling. (Advice giving is not favored by passive or affective counseling theories such as client-centered or psychoanalytic therapies.)

2. Can be used in vocational and educational counseling based on diagnostic information about the client.

3. Can be effective with American Indians who often value the advice of an experienced, wise, and/or older person (Bryde, 1971).

4. Has been effective in advising clients on academic courses, training opportunities, job possibilities, and career decisions.

Role of the Counselor

1. The counselor should be cautious in using the technique of advice giving since the client is likely to put much confidence and credibility in professional opinions and may even blame the counselor in the future for advice given that does not prove to be beneficial.

2. The counselor should (a) avoid absolute introductory statements to advice (e.g., "You must...," or "You had better..."), (b) provide several recommendations or opinions when appropriate, (c) give careful consideration to available, valid, and accurate information on which advice is based, and (d) make sure that rapport and timing are right for advice giving thus avoiding client resistance.

Limitations of Advice Giving

Advice giving can be limited or ineffective if:

1. The client has no motivation for taking action to change.

2. The advice is impractical or unrealistic for the client.

3. The counselor communicates a tone of low expectation, lack of confidence in the client, or disrespect in regards to the client's capacity to benefit from the advice.

4. The advice is based on invalid data or information.

5. The counselor does not have adequate rapport with the client.

Examples of Advice Giving

Example 1:   Direct Advice (Statement of Opinion with Explanation)

CLIENT: Do you think it is better to go to school part-time or full-time?

COUNSELOR: My own preference is to take a full college load. I think it allows more time for study and greater involvement in the learning activities of the program and university. It also results in an early completion of the degree and more opportunities for getting to know people in the program. However, I would suggest you decide for yourself based on your own financial and job situation and your own lifestyle and priorities. (In this example, the counselor gives her own opinion with perceived advantages or reasons while also suggesting the client make his own decision based on his needs and values.)

Example 2:   Advising Courses of Action (From Which to Choose)

CLIENT: I am getting frightened; graduation (from high school) is right around the corner and I haven't decided what to do with my life.

COUNSELOR: There are numerous opportunities for high school graduates today based on their interests and abilities. I would recommend that you consider possibilities such as a branch of the armed forces, college, technical training, volunteer U.S. or foreign services, government work, or a job in some industry.

As I mentioned to you in an earlier counseling session, we have information here from which you can learn about these opportunities. We also have tests that can tell you more about your abilities and interests. However, we need to act now in order to plan ahead before positions and opportunities are all taken.

References

Bryde, J. (1971). Indian students and guidance: Minority groups and guidance (Guidance Monograph Series, No. VI). Boston: Houghton Mifflin.

Ohlsen, M. (1974). Guidance services in the modern school. New York: Harcourt, Brace Jovanovich.

Williamson, E.G. (1950). Counseling adolescents. New York: McGraw-Hill.

---

021   **SUMMARIZING**

Definitions of Summarizing

- Counselor's attempt to bring together relevant, fragmented material that has been disclosed by the client during the counseling session (Egan, 1986).

- Counselor's synthesis of the essence of what has been communicated in the counseling session; also highlights of the major affective and cognitive themes (Okun, 1987).

Purposes and Outcomes

1. Serves to integrate material and to provide feedback to the client in terms of feelings and thoughts.

2. Is used as a cue to the ending or termination of the counseling session.

3. Is used at a selected therapeutic point in counseling in order to put the counseling session in perspective.

4. Provides a common understanding between the counselor and the client in regards to what has occurred; clarifies and crystallizes aspects of the counseling relationship.

Applications of Summarizing

1. Can be used in individual counseling at (a) the opening of the counseling session to summarize the previous meeting and thus provide continuity between counseling sessions, (b) the midpoint or any appropriate point in the counseling session in order to put things in perspective, and (c) the end of the counseling session to bring the session to a close.

2. Can be employed in group counseling and group psychotherapy in the same manner as in individual counseling.

3. Can be used in group guidance or orientation groups for the purpose of summarizing important points of guidance information that is presented to the group.

4. Can be used to summarize diagnostic data (including test results) to the client as well as to summarize other guidance information.

Role of the Counselor

1. Summary statements that are too long can increase the chance of counselor inaccuracies, counselor judgmental comments, and possible client resistance or fatigue.

2. The counselor should be careful not to overuse "summarizing" since it is not the type counseling technique that is prone to or appropriate for frequent use.

3. The effective summary statement should be succinct, clear, and true to what has actually occurred in the counseling relationship. Moreover, it should not be biased by the counselor's own values, beliefs, judgments, or prejudices.

Examples of Summarizing

Example 1: Summarizing at the End of a Counseling Session

CLIENT: Sorry to have burdened you today with all my problems; seems as though the whole roof is coming down on me.

COUNSELOR: That's O.K. I'm glad to try to be of help (pause). Before you leave, maybe we can try to summarize or pull things together. Like you said, of course, you have a lot of difficulties coming all at once--your grandfather's illness, financial concerns about upcoming bills this month, and a souring relationship with your child. Although that appears to be a lot, you have promised me and yourself that you will try to do something positive and constructive about each, starting with those most immediate concerns and those over which you have more control.

Example 2: Summarizing Within a Counseling Session

(The following is an example related to a group counseling setting.)

GROUP MEMBERS: (All group members become silent after 20 minutes of intensive focus on the concern of one of its members. There is an atmosphere of tension, loss of words, and concomitant flashing thoughts including reflections on what has been said, sorrow for the client's problem, and anticipation of the next possible focus of concern for the group.)

GROUP LEADER: Let me see if I can bring together what has happened thus far. For the last 20 minutes, we have attempted to help Mary with her concern about a relationship with a married man. It's like she has been torn between continuing to see him and trying to get out of the relationship. I sense that the group feels she should get out, but at the same time Mary has expressed her emotional difficulty in cutting the string--although she feels it is better to get out now. Well, I guess Mary feels that she has got some help and support based on her comments to the group and her look of appreciation (pause). Right now it seems as if some members are anticipating the next stage of the group's concern while others are still reflecting on our discussion about your problem Mary.

References

Egan, G. (1986). The skilled helper: A systematic approach to effective helping (3rd ed.). Monterey, CA: Brooks/Cole.

Okun, B.F. (1987). Effective helping: Interviewing and counseling techniques (3rd ed.). Monterey, CA: Brooks/Cole.

022   INFORMATION GIVING

Definition of Information Giving

Information giving refers to the counselor's act of sharing timely and meaningful verbal information for the behavior change and self-improvement of the client.

Purposes and Outcomes

1. Provides limited verbal knowledge at a key point in counseling for the client's insight and awareness.

2. Provides a lead or introduction to printed or audio-visual information on topics related to occupations, personal living, training and educational opportunities, tests, social adjustment, and academic courses.

3. Presents information that serves to facilitate the client's effective decision-making and change in perception or attitudes.

4. Is one of the three purposes of counseling, according to Ratigan (1972)--the other two are "getting information" and "changing behavior."

Applications of Information Giving

1. Information giving can be used for the intent of preventing client problems as well as remediating problems.

2. The type of information and the frequency of information giving vary according to the theoretical approach of the counselor. For example, client-centered counselors give little information; trait-and-factor counselors frequently share information about test results, occupations, and training; and psychoanalysts often share insightful information about the client's past or unconscious motives.

3. The counseling setting and client problem also influence the type information shared by the counselor. For example, counselors in drug abuse programs tend to share information about the effects of drugs; alcoholism counselors may counsel alcoholics about the physical, social, and economic effects of alcoholism; and financial aid counselors primarily share information about sources of financial support.

4. Information giving can be applied in the group counseling setting in the same manner as in individual counseling. Moreover, in group guidance (or information groups), it is the main technique of providing information to clients for preventive purposes (Gazda, 1984; Yalom, 1985).

5. The technique of information giving is used many times in conjunction with advice giving, usually within the context of sharing background information related to the advice (Brammer & Shostrom, 1982).

Role of the Counselor

1. The counselor should only give verbal information when it is timely to present during the counseling session or when the client requests information in connection with a problem or concern.

2. The counselor should also be cognizant not to deluge the client with too much information in one sitting.

3. The counselor may even recycle information that has come from the client (i.e., using new language or images that are therapeutic) or may choose to cautiously alter misinformation that the client demonstrates--especially misinformation that can possibly result in harm to the client.

Limitations of Information Giving

The effectiveness of information giving in the counseling and psychotherapy settings may be limited by the following considerations:

1. Is the information valid, reliable, and useful to the client? (Is the information applicable to the client's background, orientation, and educational level? Is it up-to-date information? Is the information useful in terms of the client's needs?)

2. Is it assumed that the client will take the information and use it rationally for his or her own well-being and growth?

3. Is the information presented in a manner in which it will have a maximum effect or at least achieve what it is intended to do? (What tone of voice is used? How much information is given in one sitting? What information is given? What words and language are used and are these understandable and acceptable

to the client?)

4. Is the information given at a timely point in the counseling relationship based on the client's readiness and motivation for information consumption, processing, and utilization?

Examples of Information Giving

Example 1: Giving Information Upon Request

CLIENT: Everything is going wrong at once; I need a job, my family is sick, and one of my kids is on drugs and about to drop out of school. What can I do with all these problems and no money—is there any help anywhere?

COUNSELOR: There are several places where we might get free services such as help in finding a job, medical care, and youth drug counseling. I will be happy to assist you in trying to gain these services through appropriate referrals.

Example 2: Voluntary Information Giving

CLIENT: It's good I can come in and talk to you. It is hard, you know, being a freshman; just hard to meet people and make friends.

COUNSELOR: I'm delighted that you took this opportunity for some professional assistance; i.e., to come in and talk. About meeting other students, you may want to join one of our discussion groups or counseling groups here in the university counseling center. We run them each semester; and I will be happy to explore this option with you.

Example 3: Correcting Misinformation

CLIENT: Thanks for helping me to overcome my fear of going to the clinic. I'm glad it's all over. My friends tell me if you catch it once you can't get it again; just like having the measles you know.

COUNSELOR: That is not exactly true. If you are treated for gonorrhea and later get infected by a person who has it, you stand the same chance of contracting it again. So don't be misled by rumors. Look, let me give you a free booklet on venereal diseases that will give you the facts about gonorrhea and other diseases, O.K.? Read it and we can talk about it at the next counseling session, if you want to.

References

Brammer, L.M., & Shostrom, E.L. (1982). Therapeutic psychology (4th ed.). Englewood Cliffs, NJ: Prentice-Hall.

Gazda, G.M. (1984). Group counseling: A developmental approach (3rd ed.). Boston: Allyn & Bacon.

Ratigan, W. (1972). Counseling theory and practice in the school. In B. Stefflre & W.H. Grant (Eds.), Theories of counseling (2nd ed.). New York: McGraw-Hill.

Yalom, I.D. (1985). The theory and practice of group psychotherapy (3rd ed.). New York: Basic Books.

---

023   **QUESTIONING**

Definition of Questioning

Questioning or the direct question is simply an interrogative statement that requires either a closed-ended answer (e.g., yes or no) or an open-ended answer. These two types of questions are often referred to as **closed-ended questions** and **open-ended questions.**

Purposes and Outcomes

1. Questioning or the direct question is useful especially in the beginning of the counseling relationship, in order to gain general background information and specific bits of information that clarify and fill in gaps.

2. Questioning is the primary technique employed in the interview (a phase in counseling or a form of counseling).

3. Questioning can also be employed to gain additional information for the purpose of clarifying a statement that has been made by the client.

4. The introductory word of the question tend to structure the nature of the client's answer. Some examples of such introductory words and their evoked behaviors follow:

> **When**   (yields a limited answer in reference to time of an event)
>
> **What and How**   (generate flexible and generous amounts of information)

Did, Do, Are, and Will (often yield yes-or-no answers)

Why (likely to force explanation, intellectualization, or rationalization)

Would and Could (request the client's willingness or ability to provide more information or pursue a course of action)

Applications of Questioning

1. The technique of questioning is more likely to be used with greater frequency in career counseling and educational counseling than in personal-social counseling.

2. Questioning is favored more by the cognitive or directive therapists vis-à-vis the affective or nondirective therapists.

3. Questions can be asked that would help the client to explore and understand himself or herself as well as to provide information for the counselor's understanding and diagnosis of the client (Brammer, 1988).

4. Questioning is one of the most popular and essential counseling techniques and is applicable to a wide variety of counseling situations, populations, modalities, and settings.

Role of the Counselor

1. The counselor should minimize the use of closed-ended questions since they tend to evoke limited information or one-word answers and since a series of such questions can bring about a tense and choppy interaction between the client and the counselor (Tolbert, 1982; Buccheimer & Balogh, 1961).

2. Where and when appropriate, the counselor should employ open-ended questions introduced by words such as "how" and "what," i.e., for the purpose of acquiring a generous amount of information while allowing the client flexibility of response.

3. The counselor should be careful not to overuse the technique of questioning, especially when a comparable or more effective technique can be used.

4. The counselor should be sensitive to the <u>timing</u> of questions that can be either premature or emotionally frustrating for the client if raised at an inappropriate time during the counseling relationship. Moreover, the counselor should avoid questioning that suggests a tone of interrogation or plain curiosity.

5. Questions raised by the counselor should be <u>brief</u> and as <u>clear</u> as possible, along with being timely.

6. The counselor can employ questioning in order to acquire (a) general information, (b) specific information, (c) clarification of information already presented, (d) elaboration on an answer, and (e) as a means of confronting the client about his or her behavior.

Examples of Questioning

Example 1: Closed-Ended Questions Requesting a Yes-or-No Answer
COUNSELOR: **Did** you suspect that you would lose your job?
CLIENT: No.

COUNSELOR: **Do** you often stay in on weekends?
CLIENT: Yes.

Example 2: Open-Ended Question Introduced by "What" (Evokes Content Information)
COUNSELOR: **What** happened after your husband slapped you?
CLIENT: I guess it was both shocking and embarrassing. What I am saying is that he caught me off guard. I didn't think he would hit me ever--and especially in public among our card-playing friends. I kind of deserved it--you see, I had been demeaning him all night as a cop out for my own guilt about this affair that I've been carrying on behind his back. Remember, I told you about it and all about my conflict of feeling caught between two men. Anyway, getting back to his slapping me at the party, I guess he was so hurt from my verbal abuse of him that night, those little bitchy comments, that striking me was his only recourse to retaining some type of self-respect, especially in front of the "boys."

Example 3:   Open-Ended Question Introduced by "How" (Evokes Process Information)

COUNSELOR: **How** did you come to the decision to leave your home and come all the way out here to graduate school?

CLIENT: I always wanted to get back into school and learn, you know; develop me, get out of this domestic rut.   For 20 years I've lived with this man who, like I told you, have attacked me, discouraged me, and just ignored our two kids-- rather teenagers.   I just decided it was now or never, and I felt the farthest away the university was from my former husband, the better.   I am really happy now doing what I always wanted to do; plus I get a chance to see my kids who are in college about 150 miles from here.

Example 4:   Open-Ended Question That Evokes an Explanation

COUNSELOR: **Why** do you get drunk each night after work?

CLIENT: Look, Mr. big shot gentleman with your fancy job and salary; a man got to do somethin'--with nothing but a shack, a lazy fat wife, and six hungry kids to feed.   Give me a break; what else can I do?   This is the only joy I got. (This example suggests a tone of resistance on the part of the client along with an attempt to rationalize and justify his drinking behavior.)

Example 5:   Question That Yields General Information

COUNSELOR: What are concerns that you would like to talk about?

CLIENT: Well, there is a whole lot of things pressing on my mind; maybe I should take them one at a time.   The most serious concern....

Example 6:   Question That Yields Specific Information

COUNSELOR: Are you familiar with the Occupational Outlook Handbook?

CLIENT: Yes, I used it once here at the counseling center.

Example 7:   Question for Clarification

COUNSELOR: When you say, "He was a 'bad' dude," did you mean he was some-body you liked or wanted to be like?

CLIENT: Yeah man, you got it; you got that right!

Example 8: Question for Elaboration

COUNSELOR: Could you tell me a little more about what happened?

CLIENT: It is very difficult to talk about it (pause). I had been out with him several times and I trusted to be alone with him--since he seemed so polite, cuddly, and easy to talk to. We (mild choking sound and moderate pause) kissed passionately; and then like he seemed a different person--wide-eyed, in rage, grappling and tearing at my dress (silence, then quiet tears with shame).

Example 9: Confrontation Question

COUNSELOR: How come you never talk about your weight problem in our group counseling sessions or our one-to-one counseling sessions?

CLIENT: (embarrassingly with head dropping briefly) I kind of deny it, I guess, by not talking about it and assuming it doesn't exist. Most people see it but don't mention it for fear they will hurt my feelings. I guess you have noticed that I am still gaining--my doctor says I must lose 100 pounds or run into serious health problems.

Additional Comments on the Technique of Questioning

The following observations suggest ways in which questioning can be limited or ineffective as opposed to facilitative. The counselor should:

1. Not interrupt to ask a question when the client is talking or when the client is in the middle of a deep thought during a silence.

2. Not ask questions that reflect a stereotypical bias toward a client's ethnic background or culture. (For example, a Black counselor may ask a college student of Asian background, "When is the last time you had some good Chinese food?" Or a White counselor may ask a Black client, "What is the latest popular soul dance?" These two questions stereotypically presume that all Chinese eat Chinese food and that all Blacks know how to dance and love dancing.)

3. Avoid questions that begin with, "How do you feel about...?" These type questions force the client to intellectualize emotion or cogitate on a feeling which is not usually true to the situation or his/her own emotion.

4. Avoid "heavy" questions that are asked in an accusing tone or voice. (For example, "You said your boyfriend told you that he had to be treated for V.D.; tell me, did you give it to him?")

References

Brammer, L.M. (1988). The helping relationship: Process and skills (4th ed.). Englewood Cliffs, NJ: Prentice-Hall.

Buccheimer, A. & Balogh, S. (1961). The counseling relationship: A casebook. Chicago: Science Research Associates.

Tolbert, E.L. (1982). An introduction to guidance. Boston: Little Brown.

024   **REASSURANCE**

Definition of Reassurance

Reassurance is a counseling technique that communicates a tone of support, comfort, encouragement, acceptance, and/or reinforcement to the client.

Purposes and Outcomes

1. Reassurance helps to relax the client, reduce anxiety, or motivate positive behavior or achievement.

2. Reassurance serves to support the client in a time of grief, loss, uncertainty, or low self-confidence.

3. Reassurance assures the client that things will "turn out okay" or that "life will return to a normal state."

Applications of Reassurance

1. Reassurance has broad applications for a number of counseling settings and with a variety of clients; however, it should not be overused or misused.

2. Reassurance can be applied in order to relax a client who is anticipating an anxiety-provoking event (e.g., a test, job interview, social date, or group counseling experience).

3. Reassurance can be employed to express approval of a verbal remark or an action by the client. It can also be used to predict a client's success in an anticipatory event.

4. Reassurance is applicable to client problems such as depression, misfortune, indecision, stress, conflict, and loneliness.

Role of the Counselor

1. The counselor's intent and role in using the technique of reassurance is that of expressing concern for the client's welfare along with a promise or expectation of improvement for the client (Brammer & Shostrom, 1982).

2. The counselor should not overuse reassurance but should use it in a timely and appropriate manner when there is a realistically perceived feeling that the client is in need of support or encouragement. By the same token, the importance of reassuring the client should not be overlooked.

3. The counselor can also use "postdictive reassurance" or a reassuring about something that has happened in the past of which the client may have some misgiving or ambiguity (Kelly, 1955).

4. The counselor should be cautious about the choice of words and phrases employed in a reassuring statement. For example, the counselor should **avoid** overused euphemisms that can raise suspicion of sincerity or resistance on the part of the client. Specifically, the counselor should <u>avoid</u> or <u>employ caution</u> with statements such as:

> "I understand how you feel."
> "Everything will be alright."
> "Don't worry; I'm with you."
> "Don't feel alone; many people have the same problem as you."

Examples of Reassurance

Example 1: Grief

CLIENT: I just can't go on without my mother (reference to death); she was so close to me (sniff)--like a sister. (Client is a 26-year-old woman with one child.)

COUNSELOR: You can and must. There are others you must live for and others who are living for you (soft, empathic, and understanding tone but firm, confident, and supportive).

Example 2: Anxiety about Anticipatory Failure

CLIENT: Here I am at 36, about to get married, and have never had sexual intercourse with a girl. I've got to the point where I am just too anxious to get up for trying; she might laugh if I fail or I just may not be able to get an erection or even know what to do.

COUNSELOR: I sense that this is a very difficult and important concern for you; and I want you to know that I am here to give you support.

Example 3: Reassurance by Agreeing

CLIENT: My family and classmates think I'm weird because I don't accept every date, smoke pot, and hang out at the shopping center with the gang. I just like to talk with boys who have similar interests; along with doing things like reading, playing chess, jogging, and cooking health foods. Is there anything wrong with these type things? (This is a 15-year-old suburban high school student.)

COUNSELOR: I agree that you have a perfect right, like anybody else, to enjoy those things you like to do and enjoy them with persons you like.

Example 4: Loneliness

CLIENT: My presenting problem when initially coming to you was dissatisfaction with my job as a secretary. But I guess you can tell now that the real problem is that I am lonely in this big city and I am scared to get out and meet people. I just feel so depressed sometimes--like just ending it all.

COUNSELOR: Your situation is one that many young, single women face who come to a large, urban city like New York (pause). I want you to know that you have a person in me whom you can feel free to talk. At the same time, we can work on ways in which you can meet people whom you can appreciate and enjoy.

Example 5: Postdictive Reassurance (A Group Counseling Setting)

GROUP MEMBER: I've been thinking over the weekend; maybe I should not have told the group, last session, that I am gay--maybe I could have waited. You never know how people take that type thing, how they really feel on the inside--you know?

GROUP LEADER: I sense that it was a relief for you in sharing that personal part of you; and I respect you and feel closer to you as a person for being honest and open with the group and with yourself. How do other members of the group feel?

References

Brammer, L.M., & Shostrom, E.L. (1982). Therapeutic psychology (4th ed.). Englewood Cliffs: Prentice-Hall.

Kelly, G.A. (1955). The psychology of personal constructs. New York: Norton.

025   ADDITIONAL VERBAL TECHNIQUES

The following verbal techniques are not as popular and widespread in usage as the ones already discussed. Moreover, they tend to be variations or subtypes of the major or more popular verbal techniques.

Suggestion

Suggestion is a mild form of advice giving. It often recommends a single course of action in a tentative tone.

Examples

- "You might want to take the research course before taking the statistics; however, that's up to you."

- "I would suggest that you take research first in order to get some feel for statistics; that is, since you've never taken a stat course."

Clarification

Clarification is a verbal technique that calls for the client to clarify his or her comment by providing additional information or via rewording the comment. The counselor can request clarification in the form of a question, reflection, or interpretation as a response to the client's ambiguous comment.

Examples

- "When you say 'they always give you a hard time,' are you talking about your in-laws?"

- "Let me see if I am clear; you're saying you rather quit your job than take a cut in pay and a lower job-level rating."

Encouragement

Encouragement is a form of reassurance. It provides support of the counselor for the client in an ongoing task or an upcoming challenge or action that the client is anticipating.

Examples

- "From your grades last year and your current test scores, I am confident you can make the Dean's List if you really work toward it."

- "Although it's difficult, if you are going to stand a good chance of getting employment, you will have to continue to look and use creative approaches. Meanwhile, we can provide whatever supportive services for which you may qualify-- okay?"

Restatement

Restatement refers to an actual restating of the meaning or feeling of the client as the client has expressed it. Restatement is a specific form of reflection which uses verbatim or almost verbatim language of the client.

Examples

- Client: "No matter what I try, I just can't get my head together."
  Counselor: "It's like (pause), no matter what you try, you just can't get your head together."
- Client: "I'm tired of this job and just want to get out."
  Counselor: "You're saying, 'I'm tired of this job and just want to get out.'"

Probing

Probing is the use of a series of related questions and/or statements that elicit specific answers. The counselor pursues a course of questioning and requests that rapidly bring about client disclosure and awareness while allowing the counselor to quickly zero in on a problem or concern.

Examples

- "Tell me more about...."
- "What happened the following day when...?"
- "What is the status of the situation now?"

Confrontation

Confrontation is a verbal technique that raises questions or presents feedback in order to bring the client face-to-face with a denied feeling, resistance, or a personal conflict. The counselor is straightforward but honest and nonthreatening so as not to evoke further resistance.

Examples

- "Linda, you can lose weight but it seems you have chosen not to."
- "Your doctor says your prognosis is six months to one year with your type of cancer at this stage. Have you thought much about what you are going to do with your time and life?" (Also, consider the prognosis might not be accurate.)
- "John, for several counseling sessions, you have been blaming a whole lot of people and things for your problems; but it seems to me that you are basically responsible for your own situation and only you can change it."

026   SUMMARY AND ANALYSIS OF VERBAL TECHNIQUES

Summary

This section has reviewed verbal techniques that are often cited in the literature and frequently used by counselors. The major or popular techniques discussed at length included (a) reflection, (b) interpretation, (c) advice giving, (d) summarizing, (e) information giving, (f) questioning, and (g) reassurance. The less popular or minor techniques discussed in brief were suggestion, clarification, encouragement, restatement, probing, and confrontation.

Each technique discussed in this section is summarized and analyzed in Table 6 by description, example, purpose, and type of behavior elicited.

Analysis 1   (By Type)

The "description" column of Table 6 also indicates techniques that are subtypes or variations of the major verbal techniques.   These include:

- SUGGESTION   (a mild form of advice giving)
- ENCOURAGEMENT   (a specific form of reassurance that supports the client
        toward the achievement of a goal)
- RESTATEMENT   (a verbatim form of reflection)
- PROBING   (a series of related questions)

Other verbal techniques that have not been discussed herein can also be analyzed as subtypes or variations of those presented in this section.   That is, they may overlap, differ in strength of application, be synonymous in meaning, or be subtypes of some of the more frequently employed verbal techniques.   The following are examples of such techniques.

- PARAPHRASING   (a form of summarizing, reflection, or clarification)
- ASSURANCE   (a form of or synonymous with reassurance)
- TENTATIVE ANALYSIS   (a cautious form of interpretation)
- PERSUASION   (a form of advice giving that is strong and persistent)
- GENERAL LEAD   (a form of questioning or information giving that generates
        rapport and dialogue)

Analysis 2   (By Application)

The effectiveness of applying verbal techniques in the counseling relationship is contingent upon additional factors beyond one's ability to draw from a repertory or cookbook of such techniques.   In effectively applying verbal techniques, the counselor or psychotherapist should consider:

1. Timing   (when to apply the technique)
2. Level of application   (how strongly to apply and how far to go)
3. Deliverance   (state of voice and body language)

4. <u>Nature of clientele</u> (with whom to apply)

5. <u>Nature of the counseling problem</u> (appropriateness and effectiveness of the techniques per the client's problem)

Notes

Table 6

Frequently Used Verbal Techniques

By Description, Example, Purpose, and Type Behavior Elicited

Verbal Techniques	Description	Example	Purpose	Type Behavior Elicited
Summarizing	Summing up the counseling session or a segment of the session	Let me summarize what has been said thus far. . . .	Feedback/Integrates	Feeling/Thought
Advice Giving	Recommending a course of action or alternative solutions/options	There are several things you might consider. . . .	Direction/Stimulates action	Thought/Action
Information Giving	Presenting facts or information during the counseling session	Let me share with you a few facts about. . . .	Understanding/Decision making	Thought
Questioning	Requesting information via direct question	What happened after you found out. . . . ?	Understanding/ Information/Clarity	Thought
Reassurance	Supporting and approving	I believe you can do it if you want to.	Support/Anxiety reduction/Encouragement	Action
Reflection	Feedback of feeling and content	You're saying that you feel ashamed about. . . .	Self-Direction/ Awareness/Integration	Feeling/Thought
Interpretation	Inferring meaning and cause of behavior	You seem to be relating to your wife in the same way as with your mother.	Insight/Explains	Feeling/Thought
Suggestion	Mild form of advice giving	I suggest that you sign up for. . . .	Suggests course of action	Action
Clarification	Follow-up of a comment for clarity	You mean that you will quit school if. . . . ?	To make clear	Thought
Encouragement	Support toward a goal (a form of reassurance)	I feel you can overcome your illness if. . . .	Motivation/Support	Action
Restatement	Verbatim reflection of comment	You're saying, "It's all over"? (love affair)	Awareness/Clarification	Feeling/Thought
Probing	Series of related questions or requests along the same theme	Tell me more about. . . . / What happened after. . . . ?	Specific Information/ Understanding	Thought
Confrontation	Act of encountering denied or unconscious behavior	You seem to be ashamed about the scar on your face; are you?	Self-Acceptance/ Openness/Lowering of Resistance	Feeling/Thought

Note. From <u>Dictionary of Counseling Techniques and Terms</u> by F.D. Harper. Copyright 1981 by Douglass Publishers (Alexandria, Va.).

SECTION 4

Nonverbal Techniques

027   NONVERBAL BEHAVIOR

Definitions of Nonverbal Behavior

- Behavior that includes bodily movements, gestures, and facial expressions (Egan, 1986).

- Behavior in the interpersonal relationship or interpersonal communication including or related to personal space, physical appearance, gestures, posture, body movement, facial expression, eye contact, time, vocal emphasis, and environmental factors (Heun & Heun, 1975).

Meanings and Purposes of Nonverbal Behavior

- To modify, emphasize, confirm, punctuate, modulate, or contradict a verbal message (Egan, 1976).

- To accent a verbal message, explain silence, add new information to a verbal message, or distort the verbal message (Hansen, Stevic, & Warner, 1986).

- To express feelings, regulate the flow of verbal exchange, or help one to adapt to arising needs (Ekman, 1965).

Examples of Nonverbal Behaviors

(These meanings can differ to some degree across cultural groups.)

Body Movements

1. Rubbing nose   (anxiety, indecision, puzzlement)
2. Wiggling and squirming in seat   (boredom, impatience)
3. Shrug of shoulders   (indifference, "I don't know")

4. Shaking of feet or unconscious movement (relief of muscle tension, sign of self-content)
5. Twiddling of fingers (nervousness, anxiety)
6. Adjusting necktie (show of. masculinity or superiority)
7. Slap of forehead (forgetfulness)
8. Placing hands on hips (sign of confidence, firmness, arrogance)
9. Closing nostrils with fingers (contempt)
10. Outreached arms toward another person (greeting signaling touch of hands or embrace)
11. Forming circle with thumb and finger in raised motion (O.K., "great," perfection)
12. Finger and knuckle cracking (frustration, aggression, anger, fatigue)
13. Playing with clothes or objects, doodling (impatience, boredom, preoccupation with thought or concern)
14. Brushing hands palm to palm (completion of a job)
15. Nod of head (sign of understanding of what another person is saying or communicating, "I agree," "I'm listening")
16. Ignoring a person one knows (dislike, dissatisfaction, recognition as a nonperson)
17. Scratching of head (loss of words and thought, confusion, itching of scalp)

Posture or Body Position
1. Erect head (pride)
2. Bowed head (shame, embarrassment, surreptitious anger, frustration)
3. Sitting with back to person (lack of respect, lack of interest in a person or in what the person is saying)
4. Clasped hands (isolation, alienation, aloofness)
5. Extended distance between self and another person (discomfort, intent to keep conversation brief, aloofness)
6. Arms crossed in front of chest (resistance, closedness)
7. Leaning forward in sitting position (involvement, concern)
8. Leaning backwards in sitting position (noninvolvement, intellectual aloofness, intellectual guard)

Facial Expressions

1. Tight lips, sometimes tucked with tense facial muscles (anger, disgust)
2. Dilated pupils of eyes (excited, alert, under the influence of a drug)
3. Raise of eyebrow (disbelief, shock, surprise)
4. Wink of eye, subtle smile (communication of intimacy, support, or identification)
5. Crying (joy, sadness, hopelessness, fear, lack of control)
6. Smile (pleasant greeting, experience of pleasure, mild humor that is short of laughter, apology, excuse, defense, resistance, bashfulness, coy)
7. Stare at another person (curiosity, dislike, jealousy)

References

Egan, G. (1986). The skilled helper: A systematic approach to effective helping (3rd ed.). Monterey, CA: Brooks/Cole.

Egan, G. (1976). Interpersonal living: A skills/contract approach to human-relations training in groups. Monterey, CA: Brooks/Cole.

Ekman, P. (1965). Differential communication of affect by head and body cues. Journal of Personality and Social Psychology, 2, 726-735.

Hansen, J.C., Stevic, R.R., & Warner, R.W. (1986). Counseling theory and process (4th ed.). Newton, MA: Allyn & Bacon.

Heun, L.R., & Heun, R.E. (1975). Developing skills for human interaction. Columbus, OH: Charles E. Merrill.

Suggested Readings

Dilley, J. (1971). Adding a visual dimension to counseling. Journal of Counseling & Development, 50, 39-43.

Fast, J. (1970). Body language. New York: E. Evans.

Knapp, M.L. (1978). Nonverbal communications in human interaction (2nd ed.). New York: Holt, Rinehart & Winston.

Lee, D.Y., & Hallberg, E.T. (1982). Nonverbal behaviors of "good" and "poor" counselors. Journal of Counseling Psychology, 29, 414-417.

O'Brien, J.S., & Holborn, S.W. (1979). Verbal and non-verbal expressions as reinforcers in verbal conditioning of adult conversation. Journal of Behavior Therapy and Experimental Psychiatry, 10, 267.

Schwartz, B., Tesser, A., & Powell, E. (1982). Dominance cues in nonverbal behavior. Social Psychology Quarterly, 45, 114-120.

028   PARALINGUISTIC CUES

Defined

Paralinguistic cues are nonverbal behaviors that qualify how a word or verbal message is sent or received and that include factors such as (a) tone of voice, (b) spacing of words, (c) emphasis, (d) inflection (pitch/loudness), (e) pauses, and (f) various uttered sounds. These attributes accompany verbal statements or come between words or phrases.

Examples of Paralinguistic Cues

(See Knapp, 1978 and Weitz, 1979.)

1. Artificial cough (criticism)
2. Yawning (indifference, unconscious anxiety)
3. Laughter (spontaneous response to humor or funny incident, coverup of anxiety)
4. Low voice (low spirit, depression, anxiety, lack of confidence)
5. Whistling or Humming (genuine or false confidence, joyful mood)
6. Pause between words (reflection, search for word or words, request for attention, preparation to emphasize a statement)
7. Silence (long reflection on a cue, processing of information or ideas, integrating feelings of the moment, caution, readiness to end talk or segment of a dialogue)
8. Raising of voice (anger, reaction to perceived insult, emphasizing, clarifying)
9. Stuttering or constant restatement (anxiety, sign of risk-taking behavior, uncertainty, neurological problem unrelated to psychological state or mood)
10. High-Pitch voice (anxiety)
11. Deep sigh (sign of relief from tension, fear, or an exhaustive task)
12. Swallowing unnaturally (tension, anxiety)

13. Heavy breathing (stress, anxiety, rushing, fatigue, excitement)

14. Uh-Huh (vocal expression of acceptance, "I understand," "I agree")

15. Um ("please repeat," "I don't understand")

16. Uh (sound indicating a pause between comments; a pause for thought or to search for a word or idea)

References

Knapp, M.L. (1978). Nonverbal communications in human interaction (2nd ed.). New York: Holt, Rinehart & Winston.

Weitz, S. (Ed.). (1979). Nonverbal communication: Readings with commentary (2nd ed.). New York: Oxford University Press.

029   **LISTENING: A NONVERBAL SKILL**

Defined

Listening is a nonverbal skill that requires attentive use of the sense of hearing, along with the support of other senses. It is a skill that is learned through practice and experience.

Goals of Listening (Poppen & Thompson, 1974)

- To gain understanding of the client and his/her problem.
- To provide accurate feedback to the client.
- To show respect for the client.

Things for Which the Counselor Should Listen (Benjamin, 1987)

1. How the client feels about and perceives self
2. How the client feels about others
3. How the client perceives others relating to him/her
4. The client's feelings about the counseling relationship
5. The client's aspirations and goals
6. Defense mechanisms employed
7. Coping mechanisms employed
8. The client's values and beliefs

Suggestions for Effective Listening

1. Listen for what is said, what is hinted, and what is not discussed.

2. Listen with patience and nonjudgment.

3. Avoid or minimize extraneous noises that can interfere with the listening process (such as office or hallway traffic, ringing telephone, radio, and office machines).

4. Give full attention to the client; do not divide energies between listening to the client and other competing activities (e.g., opening mail, reading memos, or small talk with passersby).

5. Be polite and considerate if an interruption is necessary. If constant noises persist to interfere with listening, attempt to make an adjustment.

6. Give feedback when appropriate to let the client know that you are accurately listening to and perceiving the conveyed message. Also seek clarification if there is any ambiguity in a message.

7. Do not interrupt the client to complete his or her sentence or to ask a question, unless there is a therapeutic justification for the intervention.

References

Benjamin, A. (1987). The helping interview (4th ed.). Boston: Houghton Mifflin.

Poppen, W.A., & Thompson, C.L. (1974). School counseling: Theories and concepts.
    Lincoln, NE: Professional Educators Publications.

---

030   **SILENCE: MEANINGS AND THERAPEUTIC USES**

Defined

Silence can be defined as a period of time in the counseling dialogue where no verbal exchange occurs between the counselor and the client. Silence should not be confused with a "pause" between words or between the counselor-client exchange; silence tends to be longer than a mere pause.

Meanings of Silence

1. Thinking and Processing (a sign of mental processing by the client or the counselor of what has been said or perceived)

2. Sign of Rejection (early in the counseling relationship, the client may perceive too much silence by the counselor as a sign of rejection or indifference)

3. End of an Idea or Discussion (frequent silent spots by the client or counselor may indicate an idea has been exhausted or the session is approaching the end)

4. Resistance (increased silence or silent spots can be a signal of client or counselor resistance that is motivated by anxiety or hostility)

5. Experiencing of Painful Feelings (an indication that the client may be working through painful emotions which are difficult to discuss or express)

6. Anticipation or Expectation (client's anticipation of the counselor's feedback or reinforcement; counselor's seeking of further response by the client or additional information)

7. Recovery from Emotional Fatigue (client's attempt to recover from an emotion-provoking thought or expression, that may often involve crying)

(For example, see Brammer & Shostrom's Therapeutic Psychology, 1982.)

Anti-Therapeutic Aspects of Silence

The following are counselor behaviors that can provoke silent resistance on the part of the client and possibly facilitate anti-therapeutic conditions in the counseling relationship.

1. Too long a silence in individual or group counseling (can cause anxiety and tension).

2. Too many silent spots or irregular silent spots (can be perceived by the client as disinterest or hurriedness on the part of the counselor).

3. Overtalkativeness by the counselor, especially in the beginning of the counseling relationship (can limit client responses and force silent resistance).

4. Repeated, unnecessary interruptions of the client's statements.

5. The counselor's persistent pursuit of a theme or problem that the client is not interested in exploring.

6. The counselor's use of a counseling theory or counseling techniques which are antagonistic to the client's cultural background, cognitive style, or interpersonal style.

Therapeutic Uses of Silence

1. The counselor should yield to silence in allowing the client to reflect on demanding thoughts or intense feelings.

2. The counselor should allow leeway for the client to untangle confusion and work through emotions while crying. Crying during counseling can often facilitate openness to and acceptance of feelings and behavior.

3. The counselor should be timely in intervening during silence with comments or techniques that are therapeutically facilitative. The counselor can allow the client time to integrate feelings and thoughts while not running the risk of maintaining too long a silence that can result in tension and loss of therapeutic opportunity.

Examples of Silence by the Client

Example 1: Client's Disinterest in Counselor's Comments/Approach

CLIENT: (Reluctance to talk; long silence with head down and hands clasped between legs; persists to give yes-no and brief answers or to say nothing except for a sigh or low-intensity vocalizations.)

COUNSELOR: It seems as if you are not too talkative today.

CLIENT: (Similar behavior is exhibited with slight movement of head and twiddle of fingers.)

COUNSELOR: You don't have much to say today.

CLIENT: (Shrug of shoulders, head is raised halfway up, and eyes quickly move up to take a quick glance at the counselor.)

COUNSELOR: How do you think I can help you today? (Counselor shifts to a direct approach to elicit a defined verbal response.)

CLIENT: (Client raises head, his eyes light up somewhat, and he gives an alert verbal response.) I need a new job and some eyeglasses.

Example 2:   Client's Preoccupation with Thoughts and Feelings

CLIENT: (After much alert discussion, the client becomes extremely reserved, reflective, and silent at different points of the session.)

COUNSELOR: It seems you made a big change in mood all of a sudden. Could you share some of your thoughts and feelings?

CLIENT: Oh, just when you mentioned "Mother's Day" coming up this weekend; I just thought--you see my mother died about two years ago when I was a college freshman. I just guess I haven't got over it yet.

Examples of Facilitative Silence by the Counselor

Example 1:   Facilitating Integration of Thoughts and Feelings

CLIENT: You made me realize what I already knew but wouldn't accept; I've been seeing this married woman, like I told you, for five years and have little control over the relationship--and I guess I don't know where it's leading to. It's becoming so frustrating and complicated. I just don't know how to get out; or maybe I don't have the desire or the strength to cut it off. (Client reflects within his own mind, cringes mildly, drops head in one hand, and begins to sob gently.)

COUNSELOR: (Silent, however, leaning forward attentively with concerned eyes and appropriate nods of understanding. Shortly afterwards, counselor touches client's hand in a show of empathy and support.)

CLIENT: It's funny that I'm able to tell you this and even feel free to shed tears. I probably never would have been this open with a male counselor.

COUNSELOR: (Nods head and smiles gently and supportively. The counselor senses the client's anticipation of a response from her and thus follows the silence with a brief comment of support.)

Example 2:   Silence for Client's Reflection and Insight

COUNSELOR: It's interesting how you have changed your attitude. When you first came in to see me about a month ago, you told me your husband was the total reason for all your miseries; now I just heard you say that you are to blame for much of what has happened to you.

CLIENT: I saw myself in the mirror for the first time last night in a different way (rapid eye blinks, deep breath, searching for appropriate expression of a developing insight).

COUNSELOR: (Silence and patience; an attentiveness in waiting for the client to further reflect in reaching a higher level of insight is expressed.)

CLIENT: I've gained 30 pounds since we've been married; I'm frustrated at home during the day with the same routine; and I'm tired of popping pills, drinking martinis, and watching dumb daytime soap operas. It seems that the years keep going by me with no growth and career satisfaction on my part and everything going for Jim (husband). (Client's eyes are fixed but unfocused on a random spot on the wall behind the counselor with one hand on her forehead while continuing to reflect.)

COUNSELOR: (Gently leans forward and blinks eyes with an attentive look of understanding and anticipation of further client expression.)

---

031   **PHOTOCOUNSELING**

Defined

Photocounseling is the use of photography, usually still photos, for the purpose of stimulating the client to reveal and explore inner concerns while simultaneously providing valuable pictorial information for counseling.

Process

- Clients use cameras to take photos of their daily activities; or clients bring in family photos or personal shots from their album or collection.

- The photos are used to stimulate discussion between the client and the counselor (in individual counseling) or they can be shared in the group counseling situation.

  (See Gosciewski, 1975.)

Purpose and Outcomes of Photocounseling

1. Yields information about the environment, family, and life of the client.
2. Provides information about the client's relationships with others.

3. Helps the client to learn more about self and his/her environment.

4. Serves as a diagnostic and evaluation technique (via photo information presented).

5. Reveals information about the client's interests and concerns.

6. Provides career experience in photography as well as a recreational activity for clients.

7. Generates enthusiasm and participation.

(See Gosciewski, 1975 and Schudson, 1975.)

Applications

1. School counseling
2. Health counseling
3. Rehabilitation counseling
4. Career counseling
5. Marriage counseling
6. Drug and alcoholism counseling
7. Group and individual counseling
8. Multicultural counseling
9. Child counseling
10. College counseling

References

Gosciewski, F.W. (1975). Photo counseling. Journal of Counseling & Development, 53, 600-604.

Schudson, K.R. (1975). The simple camera in school counseling. Journal of Counseling & Development, 54, 225-226.

032   EFFECTIVE/INEFFECTIVE NONVERBAL COUNSELOR BEHAVIORS

Effective Nonverbal Counselor Behaviors

1. **Forward Lean and Occasional Head Nod.** This body position and head movement convey to the client that the counselor is listening, attentive, interested, and involved in the total communication.

2. **Frequent Eye Contact.**   The counselor should maintain intermittent eye contact with the client to better read facial expressions, mood, and emotions along with conveying a sense of concern and attentiveness.   However, outright staring should be avoided.

3. **Ideal Physical Distance.**   A comfortable physical distance should be maintained between the counselor and the client; about 35 to 40 inches are often recommended (this can vary with the personality and the culture of both the client and the counselor).

4. **Occasional Smile and Facial Expression.**   The counselor should feel free to smile or even laugh when it is a genuine and appropriate response that is naturally stimulated; or the counselor may use facilitative nonverbal facial expressions. Some counselors feel they should not show any facial expressions at all; and thus they often communicate to the client an air of aloofness, coolness, and indifference.

5. **Gesticulation.**   The use of hands and arms in expressing ideas, describing situations, regulating client behavior, or sharing feelings may be used occasionally by the counselor.

6. **Touching.**   Touching, if spontaneous or genuine, can enhance rapport and possibly relax the client.   Touching can take a number of forms including a handshake, a supportive touch on the shoulder or hand, or a pat on the back as a message of reassurance.

7. **Eye-Movement Feedback.**   The counselor may use eye movement to bring to the client's attention an inappropriate or unconscious reaction.   For example, a client who is nervously wringing his hands while talking may become aware that the counselor is looking down occasionally at his hands such as to motion attention toward the unconscious behavior that accompanies speech.

Ineffective Nonverbal Counselor Behaviors

1. **Frowns.**   An unconscious frown on the counselor's face may communicate rejection of an expressed value, belief, or practice communicated by the client. Some counselors might frown as a sign of misunderstanding in regards to what

the client has said. However, in such cases, it should be clarified to the client so that a frown of misunderstanding will not be interpreted by the client as counselor rejection, disapproval, or disgust.

2. **Distractions.** The counselor should minimize distractions that can be disturbing to the client, such as unnecessary turning away from client to give attention to another matter. Self-Grooming, browsing through literature, glances at one's watch or clock, doodling, and other nonattentive behaviors may communicate to the client that the counselor is not totally involved and listening.

3. **Discourtesies.** Sneezing, coughing, belching, yawning, and other related nonverbal behaviors that might be perceived by the client as discourtesies should be avoided when possible or minimized and excused politely. The client expects to receive respect as a human being.

4. **Drowsy/Sleepy Behavior.** The counselor should avoid drowsy, sleepy eyes with accompanying head nods as if falling asleep. Furthermore, the counselor must try to be as alert as possible in giving full attention to each client's behavior. One way of avoiding early afternoon drowsiness is to avoid big lunches.

5. **Fidgety Behavior.** Fidgety behavior on the part of the counselor can communicate a hurriedness to get the client finished or a lack of interest.

6. **Eating.** Eating in the presence of a client can be perceived as rude and impolite, except in the case whereupon the counselor and the client may agree to have lunch and/or to meet in a place designated for eating. The drinking of coffee, tea, water, or other acceptable drinks during counseling in one's office is likely to be viewed as acceptable nonverbal behavior.

7. **Sensual Touching.** Although supportive touching and normal handshaking can be therapeutically facilitative, sensual or sexual touching could create resistance, protest, and possible legal action--if repetitive. A supportive pat on the shoulder or a gentle touch of a hand is quite different from a squeezing or rubbing touch and/or a touch on an inappropriate part of one's body, such as the thigh, knee, or hips. It must also be kept in mind that perceptions and meaning related to touch also have much to do with gender of the client/counselor, culture of the client/counselor, degree of rapport between the counselor and the client, degree of naturalness or spontaneity of the touching behavior, and the accompanying verbal behavior of the counselor.

8. **Smoking.** Cigarette or tobacco smoking by the counselor, in the presence of the client while counseling, should be avoided--especially in today's society that has become increasingly conscious about clean air and health. The counselor should not only be considerate in not smoking during counseling; but, also, in not even asking the client if he or she would mind one's smoking. A counselor's willingness to smoke while counseling can possibly impair rapport and impede the effectiveness of counseling for the client. The question of whether the client should be permitted to smoke during counseling is a case-by-case one based upon the counselor's judgment and personal preference, the client's expressed and insistent need, and/or the regulations of the counseling center or building codes as related to smoking.

9. **Inappropriate Laughter.** The paralinguistic response of laughter can be relaxing and facilitative, i.e., if the response is appropriate, natural, and spontaneous. Mutual laughter of the counselor and the client often occurs spontaneously and simultaneously as a response to expressed humor or a genuinely funny event. However, the counselor should be cautious about inappropriate laughter that can be perceived by the client as unexplained and possibly degrading and cynical. If the client seems puzzled by the counselor's lone laughter, such laughter should be clarified or excused so that the client will not perceive that the counselor is laughing at something related to him/her that is not intended to be humorous (e.g., the client's accent or manner of speech, personal views/attitudes, dress, cultural style, or physical appearance).

Notes

SECTION 5

Diagnostic/Assessment Techniques

033   DIAGNOSIS

Defined

Diagnosis refers to the identification or classification of human problems and disorders based on the observation of symptoms and the assessment of behavioral characteristics.

Purposes of Diagnosis

1. Provides a profile of the client's functioning, problems, and strengths and leads to a prognostic assessment and intervention strategy for treatment (Kellerman & Burry, 1981).

2. Facilitates the understanding of the client's behavior from an internal and external perspective, while providing a basis for treatment planning (Osipow, Walsh, & Tosi, 1984).

3. Is useful for clinicians and research investigators in their communication about disorders in common terms.

4. Is useful for planning a treatment program after assessment has been made and for comparing the efficacy of different treatment modalities (American Psychiatric Association, 1987).

Types of Diagnosis

1. E.G. Williamson's sociological type with five categories: personality, educational, vocational, financial, and health problems.

2. E.S. Bordin's five categories of sources of difficulties: no problem, lack of information, dependence, self-conflict, and choice anxiety.

3. H.B. Pepinsky's categories of sources of difficulties for student problems: lack of assurance, lack of information, lack of skill, dependence, self-conflict (interpersonal, intrapersonal, & cultural), and choice anxiety.

4. F.P. Robinson's three-category system based on the following discussion topics: adjustment problems (emotional & nonemotional), skill learning, and lack of maturity.

(See Brammer & Shostrom, 1982.)

Sources of Diagnostic Assessment (Systems, Techniques, & Instruments)
- DSM-III-R (Diagnostic and Statistical Manual of Mental Disorders-Revised)
- The interview
- Ability tests (achievement, aptitude, & intelligence)
- Personality tests
- Interest and values inventories
- Sociometry
- Anecdotal observations
- The autobiography
- The case study
- Case history
- Cumulative records
- The diary
- The essay

General Steps in the Diagnostic Process
1. Develop preliminary information about the client
2. Make tentative hypotheses about behaviors
3. Collect additional information (as suggested by hypotheses)
4. Synthesize, compare, and analyze the information
5. Reduce hypotheses (retaining the most credible ones)
6. Classify the client's behavior (if appropriate) and make predictions (prognoses)
7. Develop an appropriate counseling strategy

Cautions in the Use of Diagnosis

1. Avoid overextending yourself in the light of insufficient, incomplete, or possibly inaccurate information about the client.

2. Beware of the tendency to become too preoccupied with the history or past development of the client at the expense of neglecting present attitudes and behaviors.

3. Try to avoid the temptation to utilize tests prematurely in order to facilitate a diagnosis.

4. Be wary of losing sight of the client's individuality and becoming preoccupied with morbidity as opposed to healthy behavior.

5. Attempt to avert or minimize judgmental attitudes toward the client.

6. Try to circumvent the tendency to take too much responsibility in the diagnostic process. Allow the client to share, explore, and even "self-diagnose" vis-à-vis your making premature hypotheses based on biased questioning and limited information.

References

American Psychiatric Association. (1987). Diagnostic and statistical manual of mental disorders (3rd ed., rev.). Washington, D.C.: American Psychiatric Association.

Brammer, L.M., & Shostrom, E.L. (1982). Therapeutic psychology (4th ed.). Englewood Cliffs, NJ: Prentice-Hall.

Kellerman, H., & Burry, A. (1981). Handbook of psychodiagnostic testing. New York: Grune & Stratton.

Osipow, S.H., Walsh, W.B., & Tosi, D.J. (1984). A survey of counseling methods (rev. ed.). Homewood, IL: The Dorsey Press.

034   **THE INTERVIEW**

The interview is a dyadic process in the initial counseling relationship that involves the asking and answering of questions related to a specific, predetermined focus (Stewart & Cash, 1985).

The interview is the verbal interaction between interviewer and interviewee (or counselor & client) in which the interviewer gives of his time, skill, knowledge, and capacity in order to listen and understand the interviewee, in a way that is meaningful and helpful (Benjamin, 1987).

Opening Strategies in Interviewing

- The client should be greeted in a warm, friendly, and sincere manner.

- The counselor should spend time establishing rapport with the client in order to facilitate the client's subsequent sharing of concerns and issues.

- The counselor can use questions that focus on the client's particular, current condition; such as, "You mentioned that you are having some difficulties with your sleep; could you elaborate more on this?"

- The counselor should make more frequent use of open questions that provide the opportunity for freedom of expression as opposed to closed questions that restrict the client's reponse (Cormier & Cormier, 1985). (See the following examples of both "open" and "closed" questions.)

Examples of **Open Questions** or Invitations

"You are free to talk about anything. Could you tell me where you would like to begin?"

"What are some of the things that are of concern to you this afternoon?"

Examples of **Closed Questions** or Invitations

"What are some of the problems that you are experiencing with your history classes?"

"What difficulties are you having as related to your daughter?"

The Counselor's Nonverbal Communication During the Interview

- The maintenance of direct eye contact is recommended as a means of communicating empathy, attentiveness, and positive feelings of concern for the client.
- Head nods and appropriate smiles are expressions of the counselor's attention,

interest, and warmth—as well as reinforcement of the client's verbal expressions.

• Facing the client directly with a slightly forward lean communicates a sense of interest in and comfort with the client.

The Counselor's Role During the Interview

1. The counselor determines the nature of the client's problem or concern.

2. The counselor provides a warm and secure relationship that facilitates the expression of the client's problem.

3. The counselor assesses the client's present state of insight with regard to the problem and finds out the client's needs and interests.

4. The counselor provides structure for the therapeutic relationship, including the determination of goals and limitations, roles, confidentiality, number of sessions, and expectations.

5. In the initial interview, the counselor acquires background information concerning the client, such as previous history, family history, and current family and social situation.

6. If not handled by an agency where an administrative person is employed for such, the counselor also discusses services offered, hours and fees, and other related matters during the initial interview.

7. The counselor gives particular attention to the client's nonverbal cues which serve as useful data for assistance in the diagnosis.

(See Kottler & Brown, 1985 and Pascal, 1983.)

Physical Arrangements

• The counselor should determine the most comfortable mode of possible seating arrangements within his/her office (with and/or without a desk).

• The client should be given the freedom to sit where he or she likes or feels comfortable--within reason.

• The atmosphere should not be noisy nor distracting; neither should interruptions be the norm (e.g., telephone calls and unnecessary secretarial interrruptions).

(See Benjamin, 1987.)

Terminating Strategies

1. The client should be warned about ten minutes in advance that the session will soon end—allowing opportunity for important disclosure, integration, questions, and any summarizing.

2. No new information should be introduced at the very end of the interview session, except in cases wherein the client brings up an urgent or immediate concern that should not have to wait or be left hanging (this is usually an emotional concern).

3. The counselor might want to summarize the main points of the interview.

4. The client could be asked to summarize what he or she perceives to have occurred during the initial interview session.

5. The counselor can make suggestions for further exploration during the next interview session.

6. The counselor should leave or set aside sufficient time for discussion of plans for future appointments.

References

Benjamin, A. (1987). The helping interview (4th ed.). Boston: Houghton Mifflin.

Cormier, W.H., & Cormier, L.S. (1985). Interviewing strategies for helpers: Fundamental skills and cognitive behavioral interventions (2nd ed.). Monterey, CA: Brooks/Cole.

Kottler, J.A., & Brown, R.W. (1985). Introduction to therapeutic counseling. Monterey, CA: Brooks/Cole.

Pascal, G.R. (1983). The practical art of diagnostic interviewing. Homewood, IL: Dow Jones-Irwin.

Stewart, C.J., & Cash, W.B. (1985). Interviewing principles and practices (4th ed.). Dubuque, IA: Wm. C. Brown.

035   **ABILITY TESTS**

(Achievement, Aptitude, & Intelligence)

Achievement, aptitude, and intelligence tests are very much similar; however, (a) achievement tests are designed to evaluate past learning or instruction, (b) aptitude tests measure special ability related to a future task, and (c) intelligence tests assess general, mental or intellectual potential.

Description of Achievement Tests
- Achievement tests measure the effects of relatively standardized sets of experiences, under controlled and partially known conditions.
- They are designed to measure the effects of a specific program of instruction or formal educational learning.
- They can be used as a means of evaluating the effectiveness of a program of training or instruction.

Description of Aptitude Tests
- Are intended to measure an individual's ability to perform a task of a limited or specific kind such as clerical, mechanical, or musical tasks.
- Are designed to evaluate aptitude or ability as related to the study of specific academic subjects such as science, foreign languages, and mathematics.
- Are based on the assumption that there are specific aptitudes for specific tasks, which suggests that specific aptitudes can predict performance at specific tasks.

Description of Intelligence Tests
- Intelligence tests frequently consist of a variety of different types of test items; thus they tend to be more heterogeneous than homogeneous in content.
- Are more likely to measure general mental ability vis-à-vis specific abilities.
- Intelligence tests suggest what a person "can do," while aptitude tests indicate what one "will be able to do" and achievement tests are said to reflect what one "has done."

Examples of Achievement Tests
California Achievement Tests
Iowa Tests of Basic Skills
The Wide Range Achievement Test - Revised

Examples of Aptitude Tests

    Differential Aptitude Test (DAT)

    General Aptitude Test Battery (GATB)

    Scholastic Aptitude Test (SAT)

    Graduate Record Examination (GRE)

Examples of Intelligence Tests

    Wechsler Adult Intelligence Scale- Revised (WAIS-R)

    Wechsler Intelligence Scale for Children - Revised (WISC-R)

    Stanford-Binet Intelligence Scale

    California Test of Mental Maturity

    Culture Fair Intelligence Test

Similarities among Achievement, Aptitude, and Intelligence Tests

1. All three types of tests can be characterized as mental ability tests, implying that they reflect the effects of experience or learning as well as natural mental ability.

2. All three can be characterized as "maximum performance" tests, instructing that examinees are encouraged to perform their best within a set, timed period of testing.

3. Similar types of test items and/or very similar test batteries are often employed in the content of the three types of ability tests.

4. Although achievement tests are designed to evaluate performance, aptitude tests to predict future performance, and intelligence tests to assess overall mental ability, the three types of tests very often are used in similar manners or for similar reasons.

Cautions in the Use of Tests

1. The uses of achievement, aptitude, and intelligence tests are not mutually exclusive. For instance, performance on achievement tests is sometimes used to estimate future performance. Although such examples may be practical and sometimes feasible, the test administrator and/or counselor must be cautious to use a given ability test for the purpose of which it was designed and in accord with the directions of the test manual.

2. The testing manual for each test must be followed closely in regard to the appropriate use, administration, scoring, and interpretation of the specific ability test.

3. The meaning of ability test scores and the sharing of test results should be discussed responsibly, cautiously, and tentatively with clients. The same should apply in the case of consultation with the parents of children who are tested.

4. Counselors or test users should be familiar with guidelines set by professional associations (e.g., the American Psychological Association and the American Association for Counseling & Development) with regard to ethical standards and legal considerations related to the use of tests.

(See Anastasi, 1988; Cronbach, 1984; Fox & Zirkin, 1984; and Reschly, 1984.)

References

Anastasi, A. (1988). Psychological testing (6th ed.). New York: Macmillan.

Cronbach, L.J. (1984). Essentials of psychological testing (4th ed.). New York: Harper & Row.

Fox, L.H., & Zirkin, B. (1984). Achievement tests. In G. Goldstein & M. Hersen (Eds.), Handbook of psychological assessment (pp. 119-131). New York: Pergamon.

Reschly, D.J. (1984). Aptitude tests. In G. Goldstein & M. Hersen (Eds.), Handbook of psychological assessment (pp. 132-156). New York: Pergamon.

036   INTEREST INVENTORIES

Definition

Interest inventories are assessment instruments that are designed to measure an individual's likes and dislikes with regard to an occupation, activity, or object.

Applications in Counseling

1. Interest inventories are useful in educational and career counseling.

2. They assist the client in comparing manifest interests (those expressed by current activity) with latent interests (those indicated by their test responses).

3. They give an estimation of the client's self-concept or self-image.

4. They can be used to predict whether a client will be satisfied in a selected occupation or field of interest.

5. They promote self-understanding in the client and help to facilitate future decisions. Often, the results of interest inventories are used jointly with those of aptitude tests in order to counsel clients in their vocational decision-making.

6. They give an indication of the client's adjustment and personality style.

Examples of Interest Inventories
- Strong-Campbell Interest Inventory (for age 17 and older)
- Kuder Occupational Interest Survey (for 6th grade and above)
- Vocational Preference Inventory (for age 14 and older)
- Minnesota Vocational Interest Inventory (with considerations for lower-level occupations; e.g., skilled and semi-skilled occupations)
- Ohio Vocational Interest Survey (for grades 8 to 12)
- Work Values Inventory (for grades 8 to 12)

Future Projections Regarding Interest Inventories
- New interpretive materials, career guidance packages, and computerized software are on the increase.

- The cross-cultural use of interest inventories is increasing the demand for appropriate translations and culture-specific norms.

- There is an increased emphasis on interpretations to help maximize the usefulness of results.

Cautions in Using Interest Inventories
- Clients should be told that there are no right or wrong responses.

- Counselors should be knowledgeable of a selected interest inventory before attempting to administer it. Test reviews, test manuals, and other information should be read carefully before use with clients.

- The results of the inventory should be discussed with the client in a meaningful, tentative, and cautious manner, and should be used in conjunction with other diagnostic information about the client.

(See Anastasi, 1988; Cronbach, 1984; and Hansen, 1984.)

References

Anastasi, A. (1988). Psychological testing (6th ed.). New York: Macmillan.

Cronbach, L.J. (1984). Essentials of psychological testing (4th ed.). New York: Harper & Row.

Hansen, J.C. (1984). Interest inventories. In G. Goldstein & M. Hersen (Eds.), Handbook of psychological assessment (pp. 157-177). New York: Pergamon.

---

037   **PERSONALITY TESTS**

Definition

A psychological instrument that is designed for the evaluation or assessment of noncognitive characteristics such as emotions, motivations, attitudes, and interpersonal traits (Anastasi, 1988).

Types of Personality Tests

Projective Tests

- Usually utilize ambiguous stimuli and unstructured test figures in the form of ink blots, pictures, and three-dimensional objects. Examples of projective personality tests include the following:

  Rorschach
  Thematic Apperception Test (TAT)
  Children's Apperception Test (CAT)

- Usually reveal covert, latent, and/or unconscious aspects of personality.

- Are concerned with emotional, motivational, interpersonal, and intellectual aspects of behavior.

Objective Tests (Self-Report Measures)

- Are normally paper-and-pencil personality inventories.

- Usually have a variety of scales with assessments of a number of personality traits, sometimes on a bipolar dimension.

- The test results serve as a lead for the counselor to discuss possible problems, weaknesses, and strengths with the client.

- Examples of objective, self-report personality tests include the following:

  Personal Orientation Inventory (POI)

  Minnesota Multiphasic Personality Inventory (MMPI)

  California Psychological Inventory-Revised (CPI-R)

  Sixteen Personality Factor Questionnaire (16PF Questionnaire)

  Edwards Personal Preference Schedule (EPPS)

  Myers-Briggs Type Indicator

  IPAT Children's Personality Questionnaire

Expressive Movement Tests

- Refer to instruments to rate personality attributes via observing both verbal and nonverbal behaviors.

- For example, observations are made of the client's posture, speech, gestures, and artistic expressions.

- Are useful in revealing inner tensions, interpersonal traits, and the degree of consistency between verbal and nonverbal behaviors.

Functions of Personality Tests

1. Personality tests can provide a lead for exploring the client's problems and concerns within the therapeutic relationship.

2. They can assist in the diagnosis and assessment of the client's problems.

3. During the interview, projective tests can serve to divert the client's attention away from self, thereby reducing embarrassment and defensiveness.

4. Some projective techniques can be employed with young children in an effective manner. There are also self-report personality tests designed for children (e.g., the IPAT Children's Personality Questionnaire).

5. Projective tests are less susceptible to the faking response (of examinees) than the self-report personality tests.

6. Administered a second time, the personality test can be used to indicate possible changes in a client's personality due to treatment or counseling.

(Also, see Cronbach, 1984 and Kline, 1976.)

References

Anastasi, A. (1988). Psychological testing (6th ed.). New York: Macmillan.

Cronbach, L.J. (1984). Essentials of psychological testing (4th ed.). New York:
   Harper & Row.

Kline, P. (1976). Psychological testing. London: Malaby.

038   **SOCIOMETRY**

Definitions

Sociometry is concerned with the measurement of interpersonal preferences among the members of a group in reference to a stated criterion (Shaver, 1981).

Sociometry is a form of social mapping which reveals the pattern of attraction and rejection among members of a social group. Each member of the group usually expresses his or her choices, both for and against other members of the group. Another technique requests only positive or attractive choices in terms of first and second choices of members liked or preferred. A sociogram (or diagram) is then constructed from the pattern of choices selected by the group members (Chaplin, 1975).

Purpose of the Sociogram

1. It helps to identify individuals who may need assistance with interpersonal relationships.

2. It assists in measuring each person's social stimulus value, social worth, or personal value as viewed by associates.

3. It is used to identify leaders, social models, isolates, and rejects within a group.

4. It is particularly helpful in assessing relationships and group dynamics in counseling and therapy groups. It may also be used by teachers in assessing the dynamics of classroom youth.

Assumptions of Sociometry

1. Within any formal organization, there is an informal organization based on interpersonal attractions and repulsions; and these informal relationships affect the official functioning of the group.

2. Such interpersonal relationships have important personality consequences for each person in the group.

3. Through sociometric testing, these informal relationships can be measured and quantitatively described.

4. Interpersonal bonds between members of a group are necessary for good morale and normal personality growth for each individual.

Kinds of Sociometric Instruments/Techniques

Preferences on Specific Choice Criteria

Members are asked which persons (in the group) they like or would prefer to work with, sit by, or select for a particular activity (e.g., each member can indicate a first and second choice or preference).

Questionnaire and Rating Instruments

There are self-report instruments and scales that can be used in deriving interpersonal data for the construction of the sociogram. An example is the Interpersonal Judgment Scale in which members are asked to indicate their feelings toward each other.

What Determines Sociometric Choices

The following are factors that can interplay in sociometric choices:

1. True liking for the other person based on initial attraction or experience of reward from the other person

2. Physical proximity to the other person

3. Similarity in attitudes

4. Similarity in physical appearance

5. Similarity in social characteristics such as family background, educational level, social status of parents, social participation, and leisure-time preferences

6. Perceived cooperation with the member chosen versus perceived competition

7. The opportunity to have needs gratified by the other person

(See Berscheid & Walster, 1978.)

References

Berscheid, E., & Walster, E.H. (1978). Interpersonal attraction. Reading, MA: Addison-Wesley.

Chaplin, J.P. (1975). Dictionary of psychology. New York: Dell.

Shaver, K.G. (1981). Principles of social psychology. Cambridge, MA: Winthrop.

039   THE CASE STUDY

Definitions

Refers to a method of personality psychology that attempts to define the qualitative uniqueness of the human being. It includes a highly detailed study of the individual based on data that have been collected over a lengthy period of time (Eysenck, Arnold, & Meili, 1979).

Has reference to a form of descriptive research that incorporates material that has been accumulated over a prolonged period of time (as related to counseling, descriptive research on the client as a single case). (See Pietrofesa, Hoffman, & Splete, 1984.)

Purpose of the Case Study

- To collect information on the client that would assist in the diagnosis and assessment of problems, concerns, strengths, and liabilities.

- To generate information that would facilitate the client's exploration of feelings and development of a realistic self-concept.

- To detect areas of difficulty and weakness that need to be addressed in the counseling relationship.

- To facilitate the counselor's understanding of the client as well as the client's understanding of himself/herself.

Some Advantages of the Case Study

- It provides a profile of the whole person in terms of mental, physical, social, and emotional factors (it provides comprehensive data for diagnosis and treatment).

- It sensitizes the counselor to the numerous problems and aspects of the client's life. It can be employed with problem clients in terms of therapy and with nonproblem clients in terms of their personal growth and development.

- It can provide basic data and research knowledge for the greater understanding of specific populations of youth, college students, and adult workers.

- In schools, the case study can present a means of assisting teachers to better understand their pupils or students for effective teaching.

- The case study can draw upon other counseling techniques in order to gather the required background information on the client--techniques such as the interview, the case conference, and cumulative records.

- It can be used in career, personal-social, and educational counseling.

General Steps in the Case-Study Method (Can Vary)
- Select the client (based on the counseling concern and the need for broad-based or comprehensive knowledge per the concern)

- Determine the probable needs and capacities of the client (in order to derive the type of data to be collected for the case study)

- Collect or gather the data (using interviews, existing records, observations, and case conferences if necessary)

- Organize the data and write the report (the report can be organized by type of information discussed in the different sections)

- Use the case study report in counseling and consultation (e.g., counseling the client or consultation with teachers, parents, and other impact persons)

Content of the Case Study Report (an Example)
- Identification/Background Information (name, sex, age, cultural background, family status/history, etc.)

- Educational Information (school history, scholastic record, and psychometric test results)

- Vocational History (previous jobs held, current job/occupation, and job training experience)

- <u>Personal Data</u> (health, marital status or family's marital status for youth, hobbies and interests, attitudes, temperament, and social interests)

- <u>Miscellaneous Information of Interest</u> (e.g., based on counselor's interview, professional observations of the client, or the client's own written expressions in the forms of essay, diary, autobiographical statement, art, music, and poetry)

Case Study Versus Case History

The concepts are very often used interchangeably by counselors (Brammer & Shostrom, 1982; Warters, 1964). However, for those who differentiate, the case history focuses more on historical data and records about the client.

Limitations of the Case Study

- The case-study method can be too time-consuming.
- If not carried out in a systematic and cautious manner, there is great risk of making use of subjective sources, invalid data, or even inaccurate information. If possible, some sources or material of suspicion should be cross checked or even discarded.

- There should also be caution in the interpretation of available data for the case study, especially in terms of writing the report, communicating with the client in the counseling session, and sharing interpretations with other professional staff.

References

Brammer, L.M., & Shostrom, E.L. (1982). <u>Therapeutic psychology</u> (4th ed.). Englewood Cliffs: Prentice-Hall.

Eysenck, H.J., Arnold, W., & Meili, R. (1979). <u>Encyclopedia of psychology</u>. New York: Seabury.

Pietrofesa, J.J., Hoffman, A., & Splete, H.H. (1984). <u>Counseling: An introduction</u> (2nd ed.). Boston: Houghton Mifflin.

Warters, J. (1964). <u>Techniques of counseling</u> (2nd ed.). New York: McGraw-Hill.

040   CUMULATIVE RECORDS

Description

- Cumulative records refer to a collection of data on a student or a student's total school history—both personal records and academic performance.

- They are sometimes termed personal records, permanent records, or accumulative records.

- Cumulative records in schools often consist of a folder of facts with information that includes name, address, phone, parents, attendance records, previous schools attended, health problems/physical limitations, academic grades, test scores, job experiences, school activities (sports, organizations, etc.), and awards received.

Uses of Cumulative Records

1. They help the counselor in formulating diagnoses and in obtaining a developmental picture of a particular client.

2. They can assist the counselor in distinguishing extreme differences between standardized test data and teacher reports.

3. They save time in facilitating a quick detection of areas that need concentration in terms of a student's needs, welfare, and growth.

4. They help with making appropriate referrals if necessary.

5. They are useful for researching the effectiveness of counseling and in assessing ways to improve counseling services.

6. They serve as the basic data for case studies or case histories.

7. They serve as a primary source of information for consulting with parents.

8. They present a source of information for improving instruction and teacher effectiveness.

9. They provide information to prospective employers and college admissions offices.

(See Cottle & Downie, 1970 and Ohlsen, 1974.)

Characteristics of Good Cumulative Records

1. They contain as complete information as possible, i.e., about all aspects of the client's development and growth.

2. The information is accurate and stated objectively.

3. They are used regularly by counselors and other appropriate professional staff.

4. They are simple in organizational format and allow for a whole picture of the client at a glance.

5. They contain either annual or biannual summaries in revealing currency of data as well as developmental changes over time.

(See Bonney & Hampleman, 1962.)

Cautions in Using Cumulative Records

1. The counselor should be alert for any signs of inaccuracies in the recording of data in the cumulative records.

2. The counselor should give the client a chance to express his or her problems in his or her words before drawing conclusions from cumulative records.

3. The counselor should not jump to premature conclusions in interpreting information recorded in the cumulative records.

4. Recorded data must not be thought of as binding and final in regards to the client's behavior and ability to change.

5. The counselor should examine the recency and validity of certain types of recorded data.

References

Bonney, M.E., & Hampleman, R.S. (1962). Personal-social evaluation techniques. Washington, DC: Center for Applied Research in Education.

Cottle, W.C., & Downie, N.M. (1970). Preparations for counseling. Englewood Cliffs: Prentice-Hall.

Ohlsen, M. (1974). Guidance services in the modern schools (2nd ed.). New York: Harcourt Brace Jovanovich.

041   THE AUTOBIOGRAPHY

Definition

The autobiography is a client's written or taped inner perspectives of personal experiences or a complete life history. It is used by the counselor as a guide to significant thoughts, feelings, and events that impact the client's life while providing a valuable tool for the client's own self-exploration (Pietrofesa, Hoffman, & Splete, 1984).

Functions of the Autobiography

- It helps the client to place his/her current life situation in perspective.

- It suggests the rationale for actions taken by the client.
- It provides the opportunity for the client to gain insight into his or her inner self, including thoughts, feelings, attitudes, habits, and motives.

- It provides the counselor with valuable, supplemental diagnostic information for understanding and helping the client.

Types of Autobiographies

The Structured Autobiography

- Specific questions are asked or specific topics are designated on themes such as family history, school history, and personal history. Examples of structuring questions that generate information on the client's present, past, and future follow:

> "What kind of person am I?"
> "How did I get this way?"
> "What do I hope to become?"

- The structured autobiography yields material on a specific life-history theme or event, especially for the client who is not very verbal in the counseling session.

The Unstructured Autobiograpy

- The client is free to write without regard to specific questions or topics.

- The unstructured autobiography is designed to reveal aspects of the personality that are not expected to come out in the use of other counseling techniques.

The Comprehensive Autobiography

- The comprehensive autobiography covers a wide range of interrelated experiences over a relatively long period of time (if not the complete life history).

- Themes and topics of the autobiography are not usually limited.

The Topical Autobiography

- This type autobiography covers a specific topic, episode, or experience of one's life. It is often limited by topic or event.

Interpretation of the Autobiography

The counselor should:

- Note general impressions conveyed or communicated by the writer.

- Observe whether significant persons or events have been omitted.

- Be aware of the focus of the autobiography as an indication of the degree to which help is needed as well as the areas in which one needs help (e.g., observe areas of emphasis, topics of emotion, and lengths of topic discussions).

- Note whether there are significant gaps of omission in a chronological sequence of events.

- Pay attention to signs of evasiveness, superficiality, or attempts to mislead.

- Interpret autobiographical data in the light of other data on the client.

(See Annis, 1967.)

Limitations of the Autobiography

1. Clients can possibly refuse to disclose the whole truth, misrepresent the truth, or fail to accurately remember the true picture.

2. The validity and utility of the autobiography is dependent upon the client's self-insight, self-understanding, and memory.

3. Autobiographical data should not be used alone; but should be supplemented and/or

substantiated by other available data on the client.

4. There is risk of the client misunderstanding instructions for writing the autobiography, especially in cases of structured autobiographies and topical autobiographies.

5. The information in the autobiography can be restricted by the client's ability to communicate or write.

6. There is risk of clients denying or minimizing their weaknesses and magnifying their strengths.

7. The counselor's evaluation of autobiographical data is often subjective. (A defined system of evaluation should be considered in order to minimize counselor bias and subjectivity.)

References

Annis, A.P. (1967). The autobiography: Its uses and value in professional psychology. Journal of Counseling Psychology, 14, 9-17.

Mueller, R.J., Schieding, O.A., & Schultz, J.L. (1964). Four approaches to writing autobiographies. The School Counselor, 11, 160-164.

Pietrofesa, J.J., Hoffman, A., & Splete, H.H. (1984). Counseling: An introduction (2nd ed.). Boston: Houghton Mifflin.

---

042   **THE DIARY**

Definition

The concurrent recording of private thoughts, feelings, and significant events in a person's life (by that person), that are periodically shared in the counseling relationship (Cottle & Downie, 1970).

Uses of the Diary

- To supplement related data concerning the client's background.
- For the purpose of revealing the client's ongoing interests, goals, values, attitudes, activities, feelings, and thoughts.
- To provide a daily and weekly profile of the client's behaviors outside and between counseling sessions.

Cautions in the Use of the Diary

1. The client's diary must be treated as highly confidential material (for use in the counseling session only).

2. Since clients may not realize how much they reveal about themselves in the diary, counselors should be tentative and cautious in not going too far with interpretations and diagnoses.

3. Some clients may fantasize to a degree versus reporting real daily events and behaviors.

4. Some clients may exaggerate certain actions or feelings in their reports.

5. Information from the diary should not be used alone, but supplemented by other data when appropriate.

Reference

Cottle, W.C., & Downie, N.M. (1970). Preparation for counseling. Englewood Cliffs, NJ: Prentice-Hall.

---

043   **THE ESSAY**

Description

The essay is a counseling tool that refers to the client's writing of a personal account of his or her life or a particular aspect of his or her life. The client may have the option to write spontaneously on a topic of choice, or topics can be selected by the counselor according to an area of therapeutic interest.

Examples of Essay Topics

- "My Plans for the Future"
- "My Family"
- "Myself"
- "Things I Like to Do"
- "The Most Beautiful Experience I Have Had"
- "My Goals and Expectations"
- "My Friends"
- "My Neighborhood"
- "My Concerns in Life"

Advantages of the Essay

1. The essay is a projective technique that can reveal inner areas of conflict or concern.

2. It provides the client with an opportunity to discuss a subject close to self without focusing directly upon himself or herself as the topic of focus.

3. It allows for the written expression of difficult feelings (e.g., anger and grief) that can otherwise be difficult to express verbally.

4. It can be used to assess a person's need and readiness for counseling.

Limitations of the Essay

1. The essay is subject to the client's own attitudes, moods, and perceptions.

2. Its interpretation by the counselor can be highly subjective.

3. The counselor may be limited in knowledge and understanding of the client's culture and background, thus affecting if not outright biasing evaluation of the essay.

4. The essay may not be effective with clients who have difficulty expressing themselves in writing.

(See Brammer & Shostrom, 1982 and Shertzer & Stone, 1980.)

References

Brammer, L.M., & Shostrom, E.L. (1982). Therapeutic psychology (4th ed.). Englewood Cliffs, NJ: Prentice-Hall.

Shertzer, B., & Stone, S.C. (1980). Fundamentals of counseling (3rd ed.). Boston: Houghton Mifflin.

044　　　　　　　　　　**ANECDOTAL OBSERVATIONS**

Definition

Refer to the recognition of specific behaviors regarding a client that are recorded as they occur without the observer's judgments or interpretations (Wittenborn, 1984).

Can be recorded or unrecorded observations of behaviors in a specific environmental setting. Recorded anecdotal observations are often referred to as anecdotal records. Anecdotal observations or anecdotal records may sometimes include the observer's interpretations of the behaviors as well as recommendations (usually as a separate comment or section of the ongoing report).

Characteristics of the Written Observations

1. The written observations record critical incidents of behaviors in a given situation.

2. The actual behaviors are recorded initially without bias, judgment, or interpretation by the observer. (The counselor can serve as observer or can train a teacher or coach to record significant observations within their teaching settings.)

3. Anecdotal observations are descriptive, objective, continuous, and cumulative accounts of behaviors. They should include positive and negative behavioral accounts.

4. The content of the report is likely to include the name of the subject, age, observing situation, and occurring behaviors.

5. The behaviors observed may include actions, inactions, reactions of others to the subject (or client), nonverbal gestures/positions, meaningful verbal accounts, and any other significant behaviors. Behaviors are recorded immediately as they occur.

Uses of Anecdotal Observations

Anecdotal records:

- Furnish information about the client's personality, both social and emotional aspects.

- Assist counselors and teachers in identifying areas that need attention—in terms of student problems and concerns.

- Provide specific evidence of actual behavior as opposed to generalizations and interpretations.

- Assist in the assessment and diagnosis of disorders and needs.

- May be used as references in conferences with parents and school personnel (or professional staff in general). (Although anecdotal observations can be used in various organizational settings, they are primarily employed in the school setting.)

Types of Anecdotal Observations

Factual

These consist of a purely factual (or actual) account of the behavior as it occurs and is observed.

Mixed

These consist of factual accounts with reported comments and recommendations by the observer.

Advantages of Anecdotal Observations
- They offer continuous evidence of growth and behavior change over a period of time (e.g., weeks, months, or even years of observation).
- They offer a one-time observation of naturally occurring behavior in a chosen, natural setting.
- Information can be collected by different professional personnel who are able to observe the client from their differing professional perspectives.
- Unlike standardized tests, this technique is inexpensive to use.
- Data from anecdotal observations can be employed along with other diagnostic information as substantiation, corroboration, or even repudiation of existing findings.

Disadvantages/Limitations of Anecdotal Observations
- They can be time-consuming; demanding a great amount of work in observing, recording, and summarizing.
- Their objectivity and validity are dependent upon the qualifications and experience of the observer.
- At times, the observer may not be in a position to provide all of the essential details of an incident, or to provide occurring details in an accurate manner as they actually happen.

(See Cottle & Downie, 1970 and Shertzer & Stone, 1976.)

References

Cottle, W.C., & Downie, N.M. (1970). Preparation for counseling. Englewood Cliffs, NJ: Prentice-Hall.

Shertzer, B., & Stone, S.C. (1976). Fundamentals of guidance (3rd ed.). Boston: Houghton Mifflin.

Wittenborn, J.R. (1984). In M. Hersen, L. Michelson, & A.S. Bellack (Eds.), Issues in psychotherapy research. New York: Plenum.

045   **DREAM ANALYSIS**

A technique for uncovering unconscious material and providing the client with insight in regards to unresolved issues through the discussion of dreams (Corey, 1986).

Nature and Composition of Dreams

- Are composed of both past and present feelings, thoughts, and experiences.

- According to Freud (1955), dreams are representations of unconscious motives and conflicts, and are indicative of wish-fulfillment.

- Are composed of a manifest content (what the client actually remembers or recalls) and a latent content (unconscious material that represents hidden, symbolic, and unconscious motives).

- According to Fromm (1951), dreams are expressions of mental activity, irrational strivings, reason, and morality.

Applications for Counseling

- Dream analysis is useful in the diagnosis of oncoming mental disorder as well as in prognosis.

- It assists in providing an estimate of ego functioning.

- In Adlerian therapy, dreams are employed to assess the client's lifestyle and are interpreted as rehearsals for possible future actions by the client.

- In Gestalt therapy, dreams are acted out in the present with the creation of scripts for the different characters.

- In psychoanalysis, dreams are interpreted in terms of symbolic and unconscious meaning.

Cautions in Interpreting Dreams (Altman, 1969; Freud, 1955)

1. Dream interpretation or analysis should be done only by those who are expertly qualified to do so.

2. No one dream should be singled out as more important than another. Instead, they should all be regarded as important.

3. Counselors or therapists should listen to the dream in a neutral manner, i.e., without interjecting criticisms.

4. Analysis should be done only after the complete dream is heard and in conjunction with the client's background and experiences.

5. Counselors should be alert to any resistance, repression, transference, or anxiety in the client that might affect an objective interpretation.

6. Counselors should be tentative and cautious in sharing analyses and interpretations based on the client's dream(s).

7. The counselor should focus on repeated motifs or themes in dreams that could be indications of central concerns, problems, and conflicts in the client's life.

References

Altman, L.L. (1969). The dream in psychoanalysis. New York: International University Press.

Corey, G. (1986). The theory and practice of counseling and psychotherapy (3rd ed.). Monterey, CA: Brooks/Cole.

Freud, S. (1955). The interpretation of dreams. New York: Basic Books.

Fromm, E. (1951). The forgotten language. New York: Rinehart & Winston.

---

046   **FOLLOW-UP**

Description

Refers to efforts to evaluate the usefulness or effectiveness of formal guidance, counseling, or psychotherapy with clients. Moreover, it is a means of aftercare, of keeping in touch with clients, and of monitoring clients' progress after counseling and treatment have been terminated.

Benefits of Follow-Up

1. Follow-Up is an indication that the counselor or therapist has a genuine concern about the client's welfare.

2. It helps to provide a supportive environment for clients, after counseling has been terminated.

3. Clients are given a chance to express new problems that might have arisen after completion of counseling sessions.

4. Counselors are given the opportunity to find out whether clients were helped or hindered during counseling, in part by the client's own perceptions of whether counseling helped his/her situation.

5. Follow-Up provides clues regarding the extent to which overall treatment was effective.

(See Cormier & Cormier, 1985.)

Short-Term Versus Long-Term Follow-Up

- Short-Term follow-up produces immediate support for the client and immediate feedback regarding the effectiveness of counseling (short-term follow-up may occur over a period of one to several months).

- Long-Term follow-up provides long-term support (usually one to two years) while supplying information regarding the extent to which behavior changes are sustained despite new problems and challenges (Thomas, 1984).

Examples for Introducing the Use of Follow-Up

The following examples can be employed to introduce the idea of follow-up with the client:

1. "Why don't you give me a call sometimes and tell me how you're doing?"

2. "I always keep in touch with my clients; would you mind if I call you sometime to see how you're coming along?"

3. "Keep me informed of your progress. I'm always happy to hear from you about what you're doing."

4. "Why don't we set up an appointment so that we can review your progress and determine future directions?"

Recommendations in the Use of Follow-Up

1. Counselors and therapists should try to discourage clients' dependency on them.

2. Clients can be invited back to the counseling center for a follow-up interview.

3. An inventory or questionnaire may be mailed to the client regarding his or her progress and present status.

4. The client might be contacted by phone for an oral report.

5. If appropriate, the client might be visited at his/her home or work site.

References

Cormier, W.H., & Cormier, L.S. (1985). Interviewing strategies for helpers: Fundamental skills and cognitive behavioral interventions (2nd ed.). Monterey, CA: Brooks/ Cole.

Thomas, E.J. (1984). Designing interventions for the helping professions. Beverly Hills, CA: Sage.

Notes

SECTION 6

Adjuncts to Counseling

INTRODUCTION

Adjuncts to counseling are treatment-training activities or modalities that are often employed along with individual counseling or as part of an overall treatment plan. These activities frequently involve training (or special instructions) that result in simultaneous treatment benefits. Examples of adjuncts include biofeedback, relaxation training, assertion training, and interpersonal-skills training (or interpersonal-effectiveness training).

047   ASSERTION TRAINING

Definitions/Description

1. Assertion training involves helping the individual to express a variety of emotions appropriately, to express his or her rights without denying the rights of others, to acquire confidence to stand up for oneself, and to choose when assertive behavior is appropriate (Shelton, 1977).

2. Assertion training is a psychological intervention that trains persons to express themselves in a direct and candid manner without infringing on the rights of others (Whiteley & Flowers, 1978).

3. Assertion training is useful with clients who (a) have difficulty in saying "no" or expressing opposition, (b) cannot express anger or displeasure, (c) are too polite by letting others take advantage of them, (d) find difficulty in expressing affection or positive emotions, and (e) feel they have no right to express their true thoughts and feelings (Corey, 1986).

Assumptions of Assertion Training

- People have the right but not the obligation to be assertive.

- An individual is responsible for the consequences of his or her choices.

- Assertion is an appropriate and more fulfilling behavior when compared to passivity and aggression.

Methods Used in Assertion Training

Assertion training can occur in group counseling or individual counseling; and can employ some of the following methods among others:

- Microcounseling (brief role-played situations that often employ videotaped feedback)
- Homework (between counseling sessions)
- Audio-Taped feedback (of role-played or rehearsed behaviors)
- Peer feedback (in group counseling or real-life situations); also trainer feedback
- Behavioral rehearsal
- Modeling or imitation learning
- Bibliotherapy or bibliocounseling (books and/or printed materials with appropriate content and role-model characters)

Characteristics of the Assertive Person

1. The assertive person seeks appropriate eye contact and does not avoid the gaze of others. Neither does he or she find it necessary to "hard stare" in an expression of denial or inadequacy.

2. The assertive person insists upon what he or she feels is correct while admitting error without loss of self-esteem.

3. The assertive person is outgoing but not overbearing.

4. The assertive individual can relate spontaneously and genuinely to others at social functions.

5. The assertive individual can redress his or her grievances if necessary but can also forego redress if doing so is inappropriate or needless.

6. The assertive person can say "no" in declining a request, i.e., in a nonthreatening and appropriate manner.

7. The assertive person judges social encounters and determines appropriate responses. He or she does not attempt to hurt the feelings of others through game-playing.

(See Whiteley & Flowers, 1978.)

Applications for Special Problems and Populations
- Is especially applicable with suicidal and depressed clients, women, racial minorities, and the elderly or aged.
- Can be useful with problems concerning alienation, interpersonal anxiety, loneliness, sexual dysfunction/inhibition, and job interviewing.
- Is useful with youth and adults who exhibit inappropriate social behavior due to social learning and background.

Miscellaneous Comments on Assertion Training
- Assertion training is sometimes used interchangeably with the concepts of "assertiveness training" and "assertive training."
- The behavior-therapy technique of positive reinforcement usually accompanies methods of and client progress during assertion training.
- The procedures or steps of assertion training often include (a) identifying the inappropriate behaviors and the situations in which they occur, (b) assisting the client in understanding inappropriate versus appropriate (or assertive) behaviors, (c) identifying assertive behaviors to be learned and engaging the client in rehearsal, training, and/or practice techniques, and (d) reinforcing and monitoring assertive behavior changes.

References
Corey, G. (1986). Theory and practice of counseling and psychotherapy (3rd ed.). Monterey, CA: Brooks/Cole.

Shelton, J.L. (1977). Assertive training: Consumer beware. Journal of Counseling & Development, 55, 465-468.

Whiteley, J.M., & Flowers, J.V. (1978). Approaches to assertion training. Monterey, CA: Brooks/Cole.

048   **BIOFEEDBACK TRAINING**

Definitions
- Refers to the use of therapeutic procedures with electronic or electromechanical instruments in order to measure and provide feedback to clients about their normal and abnormal neuromuscular and autonomic activity, with the aim of developing greater awareness of and control over physiological processes (Olson, 1987).

- Biofeedback is a physiological process wherein a person learns to monitor and control his/her responses through electronic devices and thus facilitating optimal functioning and healthier well-being (Blanchard & Epstein, 1978).

The Functions of Biofeedback

Biofeedback helps the client:

- To gain mastery over aspects of behavior, especially psychophysiological responses

- To control performance by observing and acting upon previous responses

- To exercise control over nervous system activities related to physical well-being

- To relax via the reduction of anxiety and tension

- To control body temperature, heart rate, pain sensation, muscle tension, blood pressure, and other body responses and processes once thought to be autonomic

- To prevent numerous diseases caused or influenced by stress

Basic Mechanisms of Biofeedback

- The detection and amplification of the physiological response.
  Such responses of detection and amplication can be indicated by the activity of certain body processes such as brain waves and heart rate.

- The conversion of the amplified signal to an easily understood or easily processible form (i.e., for human processing).
  For example, the amplified electronic impulses are converted into auditory and visual signals such as varying pitches and digital readouts.

- Immediate feedback to the subject.
  With immediate feedback, clients learn to develop control of designated biological responses.

Applications of Biofeedback for Counseling

- The counselor or therapist can train the client to regulate psychophysiological responses when such responses can be detrimental to healthy functioning.

- Clients can be helped to monitor feelings and sensations while gaining skills in self-control.

- The counselor can assist clients to discriminate among situations and responses that require self-control.

- Biofeedback can be used to prevent stress-related problems and to enhance human performance and productivity.

Cautions in the Use of Biofeedback

- Biofeedback mechanical instruments or technology should not be employed without professional instruction and supervision.

- Therapeutic trainers should be competent and well qualified and should have some basic background of learning theory and psychophysiology.

- Clients or trainees should not expect immediate and exaggerated outcomes from biofeedback training.

- After sufficient mastery of biofeedback techniques, clients should continue periodic training and practice in order to maintain necessary gains—or they can risk setbacks.

(See Brown, 1974.)

References

Blanchard, E.B., & Epstein, L.H. (1978). A biofeedback primer. Reading, MA: Addison-Wesley.

Brown, B. (1974). New mind, new body: Bio-Feedback directions for the mind. New York: Harper & Row.

Olson, R.P. (1987). Definitions of biofeedback. In M.S. Schwartz & Associates (Eds.), Biofeedback: A practitioner's guide. New York: The Guildford Press.

049   INTERPERSONAL SKILLS TRAINING

Definitions

1. Involves training for the improvement of interpersonal effectiveness and focuses on skills such as listening, assertiveness, cooperation, problem-solving, self-disclosing, anxiety-reduction, and trust-building.

2. Refers to training related to the use of therapeutic conditions such as empathy, warmth, respect, positive regard, and genuineness in order to facilitate effective communication and understanding in the therapeutic relationship (Carkhuff & Berenson, 1977).

The Importance of Good Interpersonal Skills

1. They enhance trust in interpersonal relationships.

2. They promote a partnership between an informed provider and an equally informed consumer. (This partnership has reference to counseling relationships as well as other service-providing relationships.)

3. They favor cooperation rather than competition, sharing as opposed to divisiveness, and coordination versus unnecessary replication.

4. Interpersonal skills are useful in coping effectively with common interpersonal problems that include distressed clients, other difficult clients, group (or team) conflict, parent-child conflict, marital conflict, and everyday interpersonal conflict between professional staff.

5. Interpersonal skills are effective in high-stress helping situations such as drug programs, alcoholism treatment programs, health treatment settings, and psychiatric or mental health counseling settings.

   (See Gerrard, Boniface, & Love, 1980.)

Examples of Useful Interpersonal Skills

   Attending Skills. Preparing (for counseling or interpersonal contact), observing (especially nonverbal behaviors), listening, and nonverbal positioning by counselor/helper (Carkhuff & Anthony, 1979).

   Facilitative Skills. Reflection, restatement, and interpretation.

Supportive Skills. Approval, reassurance, encouragement, and acceptance.

Problem-Solving Skills. Direct questions, information-giving, clarification, decision-making, active listening, feedback, and goal-identification.

Assertion Skills. Oppositional skills (learning to say "no"), initiating, expressing positive and negative feelings, nonthreatening confrontation, and self-disclosure.

The Values of Interpersonal Skills to Counseling

Effective interpersonal skills contribute to:

1. Gathering data and formulating an accurate diagnosis.

2. Promoting confidence in clients.

3. Establishing and maintaining the trust of clients in the counselor.

4. Reducing clients' resistance to therapy.

5. Providing clear explanations of clients' problems and assisting in the tension reduction of clients.

6. Avoiding and/or minimizing negative reactions from the client, especially negative nonverbal reactions.

References

Carkhuff, R.R., & Anthony, W.A. (1979). The skills of helping. Amherst, MA: Human Resource Development Press.

Carkhuff, R.R., & Berenson, B.G. (1977). Beyond counseling and therapy (2nd ed.). New York: Holt, Rinehart & Winston.

Gerrard, B.A., Boniface, W.J., & Love, B.H. (1980). Interpersonal skills for health professionals. Reston, VA: Reston Publishing.

---

050   **HYPNOSIS**

Origin and Nature of Hypnosis

1. Work in hypnosis originated with Franz Anton Mesmer (1734-1815) and developed through subsequent works of James Braid in England (who coined "hypnotism") and Jean Martin Charcot in France (Watson, 1978).

2. Hypnosis is an altered state of consciousness induced by a variety of techniques and characterized generally by deep relaxation, increased susceptibility to hypnotic suggestion, and alterations in self-control and motivational level (Udolf, 1987).

Some Misconceptions about Hypnosis

1. It is not true that gullible or weak-minded clients make better hypnotic subjects as compared to the intelligent and disciplined. The ability of a person to concentrate on one object or event (e.g., reading, nature, or music) is a good predictor of hypnotizability.

2. The hypnotized cannot be made to do things while under the influence of hypnosis that are seriously opposed to his or her will or beliefs.

3. Individuals do not lose total awareness during hypnosis. In an altered state of consciousness, they are intuitively aware, more focused to the hypnotist's cues, and in a trance-like state.

4. Dehypnosis is not a problem since both the subject and the hypnotist can bring about dehypnosis.

(See Atkinson, Atkinson, & Hilgard, 1983; and Kroger, 1977.)

Applications for Counseling

1. Hypnosis is relatively effective in treating extreme anxiety, chronic conversion disorders, phobias, compulsive disorders, addictions, and problems with pain.

2. It has been associated mainly with the psychodynamic therapies; however, the behavior therapists often use hypnosis in order to relax the client and for the purpose of deriving behavioral reinforcers.

3. It is an adjunct employed in Lazarus' (1981) multimodal therapy.

4. It has been used in educational settings as a learning aid and as a technique for reducing test anxiety.

5. Hypnosis can be employed for self-improvement in social and business functioning as well as in other areas of human performance.

Cautions in the Use of Hypnosis

1. The counselor should not promise more than can be realistically accomplished with the use of hypnosis.

2. Clients should be warned that results are dependent upon their cooperation and willingness.

3. Inexperienced practitioners must not attempt to elicit deeply repressed and traumatic material until properly trained to do so, or else the client can develop "traumatic insight." Moreover, those with no acceptable training in hypnosis should not attempt hypnotism in any situation or at any level.

4. The inexperienced hypnotist should have an experienced supervisor present when hypnotizing certain difficult clients, such as emotionally disturbed persons, psychotic clients (or those predisposed), and psychopathic individuals.

5. Posthypnotic suggestions should be given so that hypnosis can be readily reinduced.

6. Ethical codes adopted by the acceptable hypnotic associations must be observed and practiced.

References

Atkinson, R.L., Atkinson, R.C., & Hilgard, E.R. (1983). Introduction to psychology (8th ed.). New York: Harcourt Brace Jovanovich.

Kroger, W.S. (1977). Clinical and experimental hypnosis in medicine, dentistry, and psychology. New York (also Philadelphia): J.B. Lippincott.

Lazarus, A.A. (1981). The practice of multimodal therapy. New York: McGraw-Hill.

Udolf, R. (1987). Handbook of hypnosis for professionals. New York: Van Nostrand Reinhold.

Watson, R.I. (1978). The great psychologists (4th ed.). New York: J.B. Lippincott.

---

051   **RELAXATION TRAINING**

Defined

Relaxation training, sometimes referred to as "relaxation techniques" or "relaxation therapy," is a step in Joseph Wolpe's (1977) systematic desensitization and involves techniques for the purpose of reducing tension, usually muscle tension. In general, relaxation techniques can be used for reducing anxiety, tension, and stress-induced responses.

Background and Nature

1.   Relaxation training was pioneered by Jacobson (1934, 1938) and, more recently, popularized by the works of Wolpe (1977) and Lazarus (1981).

2.   Relaxation training focuses on reducing tension and anxiety via relaxing different muscle groups of the body.

3.   The psychological principle of relaxation training is that the client is introduced to a positive response (relaxation) that is incompatible with an undesirable and/ or anxiety-provoked response.

4.   The methods of training can involve (a) a sequence of verbal instructions by the therapist, (b) audio, tape-recorded instructions, or (c) self-practice at home by the client (i.e., after sufficient orientation and training).

Techniques of Relaxation Training

1.   The state of the client during relaxation training can be described as (a) sitting comfortably in a quiet room, (b) keeping the eyes closed through relaxation exercises, (c) breathing deeply and slowly in a relaxed manner, and (d) tensing and relaxing different muscle groups based upon verbal instructions by the therapist.

2.   Muscle groups of focus include the arms, head, face, neck, shoulders, back, chest, abdomen, buttocks, thighs, and legs.

3.   The sequence of instructions by the therapist often calls for the client to (a) tighten a muscle or muscle group, (b) notice the sensation in the tightened muscle group, (c) gradually loosen the tension in the muscle(s), (d) notice the decreasing sensation in the muscle(s), (e) relax the muscle or muscle group completely (a "letting go") and feel the relaxed sensation, and (f) relax the entire body and feel the relaxed sensation. (This routine is usually repeated for each muscle group that is relaxed.)

Applications and Implications

1.   Relaxation training can be applied with clients who are predisposed to be tense, under situational stress, or highly anxious.

2.   Relaxation techniques can be employed in (a) the individual counseling setting, (b) group counseling, (c) a workshop training session, and (d) as homework for the client between counseling sessions.

3. Relaxation sessions can run from 15 to 20 minutes for home practice and 30 minutes to an hour for group or workshop training.

4. Although there is no sequence for muscles relaxed, instructions often start with the arm muscles, move to the head and face area, and then proceed from the neck-shoulder area to the lower limbs (Wolpe, 1977).

5. Relaxation training has applications and value for both clients and therapists. Actual training can involve one orientation session (followed by individual practice at home or work) or a series of training sessions under the supervision of a skilled therapist or instructional tape recordings.

References

Jacobson, E. (1934). You must relax. New York: Whittlesey House.

Jacobson, E. (1938). Progressive relaxation. Chicago: University of Chicago Press.

Lazarus, A.A. (1981). The practice of multimodal therapy. New York: McGraw-Hill.

Wolpe, J. (1977). Training in relaxation. In S.J. Morse & R.I. Watson, Jr. (Eds.), Psychotherapies: A comparative casebook (pp. 295-298). New York: Holt, Rinehart & Winston.

---

052   ART THERAPY

Defined

Art therapy refers to the use of pictured projections or creative images with clients for the purposes of uncovering unconscious thoughts and feelings, gaining diagnostic insight, and encouraging emotional expression (Ullman, 1975).

Functions of Art Therapy

- For those clients who deny or repress certain feelings, art therapy can assist to uncover and understand those feelings.

- Art therapy is helpful with clients who are not very verbal in expressing their feelings, mood, and thoughts.

Advantages of Art Therapy

1. Art therapy permits direct expression of dreams, fantasies, and other inner experiences that occur as images rather than words.

2. Pictured projections of unconscious material are less likely to be censored as compared to verbal expressions; therefore, enhancing the therapeutic process.

3. Artistic drawings are durable and unchanging. Their content cannot be erased from memory, denied, or altered.

4. The process of artistic expression is within itself therapeutic for the client, especially in terms of a means of releasing emotions or catharting.

Techniques Used in Art Therapy

Automatic Drawing (Scribble Technique)

The client is encouraged to draw lines or scribble on the paper. Sometimes with the eyes closed or with the nondominant hand, the client is instructed not to take his or her hand off the paper until finished. This technique allows for the release of spontaneous images from the unconscious mind. The therapist analyzes the drawings for suggestive patterns, shapes, forms, or repeated themes.

Free Drawing

With this technique, the client is absolutely free to draw anything. This technique serves as a diagnostic device and helps to reveal or confirm problems, defenses, interests, or strengths.

Color Exploration

Color exploration is used in order to assess personality organization or disorganization as determined by an integration or lack of integration of colors. Clients are sometimes advised to counterbalance selected colors with suggested ones in order to change negative feelings expressed.

Draw Your Family

This technique helps to reveal the dynamics of the client's family. Clients may draw their original family, extended family, acquired family (through marriage and/or adoption), or ideal family.

Three Wishes

The clients is requested to draw a picture that reflects three wishes. This technique serves to reveal the client's breadth of ideas, level of maturity, and degree of egocentricity. Drawings usually depict desires for objects or security among other themes. Upon completion of the drawing, the counselor discusses with the client the level of desire for the wishes to be fulfilled, the degree to which the client feels the wishes are obtainable, and the means by which the wishes can be obtained or achieved (if realistic).

Limitations of Art Therapy

1. Art therapy alone can not and should not be used as a substitute for psychotherapy.

2. Artistic responses alone, as diagnostic or therapeutic information, should not be exaggerated or generalized beyond its true significance.

3. Criteria for evaluating creative art should not be confused with criteria for evaluating the therapeutic significance of artistic expression.

4. Art therapists and counselors using art therapy should be competent in the understanding of the expressive possibilities and therapeutic value of artistic expression before attempting to make interpretations and therapeutic interventions based on such expressions.

(See Denny, 1969; Gantt, 1979; and Ullman, 1975.)

References

Denny, J.M. (1969). An art therapy workshop for the staff of a university counseling center. American Journal of Art Therapy, 9, 25-31.

Gantt, L. (1979). The other side of art therapy. American Journal of Art Therapy, 19, 11-18.

Ullman, E. (1975). Art therapy: Problems of definition. In E. Ullman & P. Dachinger (Eds.), Art therapy in theory and practice. New York: Schocken Books.

053   MUSIC THERAPY

Definitions
- Music therapy refers to the use of music in the therapeutic process for the specific purpose of arousing particular feelings within the client in order to facilitate therapy and harmonize tension states (Schulberg, 1981).

- Music therapy is the controlled use of music in the treatment of clients who are experiencing physical or emotional problems (Alvin, 1975).

Therapeutic Value of Music
- Music can evoke responses such as curiosity, alertness, relaxation, pleasure, satisfaction, self-confidence, emotional release, and enthusiasm.

- It can create an atmosphere for the client to reveal his or her problems, obsessions, mood, values, and inner thoughts.

- Music can help to uncover unconscious attitudes or to bring out memories and feelings that are hidden below the surface of conscious functioning.

Uses of Music Therapy in Groups
- Music can be used to set a mood for group discussion of a theme or topic.

- It can be employed to encourage imagination and creativity within the group setting.

- It can be used to facilitate sharing and feedback by silent members of the group.

- Music can be used to relax the group, facilitate discussion of the past (nostalgic music), minimize sadness and depression (positive, lively, and upbeat music), generate motivation for study and work, and stimulate calm and peace.
- Music can also be employed to set the stage for role playing, psychodrama, and other therapeutic group exercises.

Limitations in the Use of Music Therapy
- The benefits of music therapy can be limited with clients who have a technical or formal training background in music.

- Music therapy can be limited with persons who just do not favor music or those who have had unfavorable experiences associated with a type of music or certain musical selections. (This circumstance could either be antitherapeutic or a source of focus for counseling or therapy.)

- The counselor should not plan the listening program ahead of time, necessarily, but should try to choose selections in keeping with the current mood of the client(s) or the theme of concern.

- Material used for music therapy should be of a high standard for both musical and psychological reasons. Musical sounds can be pleasurable and pleasant or can induce irritability—especially if the quality of sound is poor and the client is nervous and tense.

References

Alvin, J. (1975). Music therapy. New York: Basic Books.

Schulberg, C.H. (1981). The music therapy sourcebook. New York: Human Services Press.

Notes

054   POETRY THERAPY
                                       (Or **Psychopoetry**)

Definition/Description

   Poetry therapy or psychopoetry refers to the use of poems or poetic verse in
counseling and therapy as a means of (a) facilitating awareness and insight, (b) improving communication between client and counselor or client and significant others, (c)
conveying feelings, (d) generating catharsis, (e) exploring values, attitudes, and self-
understanding, (f) stimulating therapeutic action and positive growth, and (g) minimizing burnout in helping professionals (Gladding, 1979; Schloss, 1976).

Methods and Techniques of Psychopoetry

1. Share therapeutic poems with the client (or a single poem that is appropriate).
   The theme of a poem should be related to the problem or concern of the client.
   Discuss poems with the client in a way so as to facilitate the client's exploration of
   feelings, attitudes, and/or values.

2. Read an appropriate poem to or with the client, or have the client read aloud a
   chosen poem that is therapeutic or educational for the moment or concern.

3. If convenient, provide copies of poems that clients can take with them for reading,
   reflection, and meditation, i.e., during their spare time between sessions.

4. If the client is inclined, encourage him/her to write a poem or poems in order to
   free up feelings and attitudes--discuss these during the counseling session.

5. Present and discuss therapeutic poems in group counseling (or have members share
   their poetry) that are related to themes or issues of the group (e.g., themes related
   to loss, anger, identity, stress, anxiety, meaning, love, loneliness, family, and relationships).

6. Provide psychopoetry in the form of printed personal-social information, audio-
   cassette tapes, or video media.

7. Consult with school and college teachers about employing therapeutic poems in the
   classroom for the purposes of values orientation and attitudinal exploration.

8. Encourage the sharing of positive and therapeutic poetry through media such as
   poetry readings, bulletin boards, newsletters, and television/radio programs related
   to mental health and human living.

Examples of Therapeutic Poems and Verse (Harper, 1985)

(POEM RELATED TO **VALUES**)

It's not so important to be liked,
  But to like yourself;
It's not so important to be good,
  But to be better;
It's not so important to receive respect
  From others, but to earn respect
  For yourself;
It's not so important to spend money
  On a person, but to spend time
  With a person;
It's not important to be important,
  But to be appreciated.

(POEM RELATED TO **LOSS/GRIEF**)

To lose is to have had;
One cannot lose a loved one
  Without falling in love,
Or lose a spouse without the experience
  Of marriage, or a child
  Without the creation or adoption
  Of life;
We can lose one's presence,
  But never the images of or
  Experiences with that one;
We can lose a loved one's presence,
  But not our memories of that one—
  Not until we lose ourselves;
To lose is to have had;
To lose is still to have.

(POEM RELATED TO **HEALTH**)

There are many rules to the good life,
  Among them is avoiding danger and
  Strife; also, it's more than wise
  To maintain regular exercise;
Swim, or run, or walk each week,
While watching daily how much you eat;
Lower your diet in salt and fat, and
Drink healthy liquids to keep your inside
  Wet;
Sing, dance, laugh, and enjoy good play,
  But work, rest, and relax each day;
Live long, live well,
  Minimize your hurry and stress;
Live long, live well,
  Keep your body at its best.

(POEM RELATED TO **FRIENDSHIP**)

A friend is special for you
  And not against you;
Being a friend is in one's state of mind;
  One's state of action—
That special one who thinks and acts
  For another's happiness,
  For another's welfare;
Being a friend is giving of self with joy;
Being a friend is receiving from another
  With appreciation;
Being a friend is wanting to be a
  Friend.

Examples...(Continued)

(POEM RELATED TO **SELF-CONCEPT**)

Everyone is special at something,
Everyone is special for something;
Anyone can be a star in one's own world,
One's own constellation, one's own galaxy;
Therefore, seek stardom and find your star,
Find your star and be a star--
    And thus shine in your own light;
Find your star and shine for you;
Remember, everyone is special at
    Something, everyone is special for
    Something--
And you are special too.

(POEM RELATED TO **ANGER**)

If you are angry, don't curse the empty
    Spaces, or damage things or self, or
    Hurt somebody; don't retaliate, or
    Mayhem, or kill--
    Just because you've been hurt.
If you are angry, don't pout, or blame,
    Or resist understanding and clarification;
If you are angry, try not to be angry
    In order to do right and just for you.
If you are angry, just close your eyes
    And breathe deeply and slowly;
If you are angry, just try to cool down
    And think straight.

EXAMPLES OF **THERAPEUTIC VERSES**

Don't wait for things to happen, make them happen.

§§§

Survival is a skill; growth is a sophisticated skill.

§§§

You can't do wrong by doing right.

§§§

It's easy to criticize; but it's difficult to perform.

§§§

Loss of affection is not just a personal experience; it is a human experience.

§§§

Free your mind, and your body will follow.

§§§

Just as a flower, each life blooms only once.

§§§

Improve your life by simply improving your attitude.

§§§

We must do what we must do, as much as we love those who love us.

§§§

True self-esteem comes from self-respect and earned achievement; it cannot be purchased or acquired undeservedly.

§§§

I can never be you; and you can never be me. But we can be we; we can be one.

References

Gladding, S.T. (1979). The creative use of poetry in the counseling process. Journal
of Counseling & Development, 57, 285-287.

Harper, F.D. (1985). Poems on love and life. Alexandria, VA: Douglass Publishers.

Schloss, G.A. (1976). Psychopoetry. NY: Grossett & Dunlap.

Notes

055   SUMMARY

Table 7

Summary of Adjuncts to Counseling

Adjunct	Purpose	Methods
Assertion Training (Or Assertiveness Training)	Facilitate expression of opposition, one's rights, & true feeling	Rehearsal, microcounseling, homework, modeling, feedback, & bibliotherapy
Biofeedback	Gain self-control & control of body responses	Electronic/mechanical feedback of physiological responses, electrical monitoring, human feedback
Interpersonal Skills Training	Improve interpersonal effectiveness	Training in attending, supportive, facilitative, problem-solving, & assertion skills
Hypnosis	Improve relaxation, susceptibility to suggestion, motivational level, & self-control	Concentration on one object-- usually facilitated by the hypnotist
Relaxation Training	Reduce tension; muscle relaxation	Tape-Recorded instructions for muscle-group relaxation; also breathing exercises
Art Therapy	Uncover feelings, moods, & thoughts; catharsis	Free drawing, scribbling, color exploration, "draw your family," & "three wishes"
Music Therapy	Reduce tension; arouse designated feelings	Use of music in group counseling as well as individual counseling (also, role playing)
Poetry Therapy (Or Psychopoetry)	Insight, catharsis, exploration of values, & attitudes; facilitate action	Sharing poetry & verse with client, writing of poems by client, & bibliotherapy (poem books)

SECTION 7

Group Counseling

056   **BASIC CONCEPTS OF GROUPS**

Group Counseling Defined

Counseling in a group setting with two or more clients. In a broader sense, group counseling refers to a variety of group methods in counseling, including various growth groups and therapy groups (Harper, 1981; Ohlsen, Horne, & Lawe, 1988).

Group Guidance, Group Counseling, and Group Psychotherapy

GROUP GUIDANCE: Information groups for the purpose of prevention and growth.

GROUP COUNSELING: Counseling groups for the purpose of prevention and remediation.

GROUP PSYCHOTHERAPY: Therapy groups for the purpose of remediating problems. (E.g., see Gazda, 1984, p. 6.)

Growth Groups Versus Task-Oriented Groups

GROWTH GROUPS: Groups designed to facilitate personal growth for members; e.g., group counseling, encounter groups, and marathon groups.

TASK-ORIENTED GROUPS: Groups established for the completion of a designated task; e.g., a committee.

Open Versus Closed Groups

OPEN GROUP: A group that is open to new members during the course of its meetings.

CLOSED GROUP: A group that is closed to new members once started; thus, not allowing any new members to join.

Group Leadership Styles

AUTHORITARIAN LEADER: Decision-Making and group power rest primarily with the group leader.

DEMOCRATIC LEADER: Decision-Making and group power are derived primarily from the group members.

LAISSEZ-FAIRE LEADER: This leadership style provides for highly unstructured freedom for leadership participation within the group.

Content Versus Process

CONTENT: The **"what"** of the group or the topics, themes, or task discussed.

PROCESS: The **"how"** of the group or the procedures, methods, or techniques by which the group achieves its goals.

Other Group Concepts

1. Group Dynamics. An area of sociological study (or social psychology) that examines relationships or interactive variables within a group.

2. Leaderless Group. Groups established without a designated or assigned leader, often designed to assess emerging leadership within a group.

3. Sociometry. A technique of measuring interpersonal preferences among group members, based upon a given personality criterion. The sociogram is a diagram that results from the technique of sociometry.

4. Feedback. Honest, open, and accurate feedback to a group member about some aspect of his or her behavior and its effect on you. Feedback should be descriptive (not evaluative), specific (not general), solicited by a member (preferred to imposed), and well-timed.

5. Common Problems Group. A group in which all members have the same concern or problem (e.g., sexual identity, academic study, choosing a career, adjustment to college, and male-female relations).

6. T-Group. T-Group represents the phrase "training group" as pioneered by the National Training Laboratory (NTL). The T-Group is an unstructured growth group designed to promote personal awareness and development.

7. Encounter Group. The "basic encounter group" was pioneered by Carl Rogers (1970) to emphasize personal growth, exploration of feelings, and improved interpersonal relationships.

8. Marathon Group. A sensitivity group or growth group designed to run from 10 hours up to an entire weekend, thus providing intense training in order to break down defenses and yield immediate awareness and behavior change.

9. Discussion Group. A group that explores and assesses the various aspects of an issue or problem with no expected plan or action on the part of its members.

10. Psychodrama. A role-played scene or theme for the client's understanding, exploration, and resolution of a personal problem.

11. Sociodrama. A role-played scene whereby persons assume roles in playing out and understanding a social problem and its dynamics.

References

Gazda, G.M. (1984). Group counseling: A developmental approach (3rd ed.). Boston: Allyn & Bacon.

Harper, F.D. (1981). Dictionary of counseling techniques and terms. Alexandria, VA: Douglass.

Ohlsen, M.M., Horne, A.M., & Lawe, C.F. (1988). Group counseling (3rd ed.). New York: Holt, Rinehart & Winston.

Rogers, C.R. (1970). Carl Rogers on encounter groups. New York: Harper & Row.

---

057   **A CLASSIFICATION OF GROUP MODELS**

The following is a classification of various group models and types based upon given dimensions for the common groupings.

I. GROUPS DICHOTOMIZED BY GOALS/PURPOSE

    1. Growth groups

    2. Task-Oriented groups

II. GROUPS TRICHOTOMIZED ON A CONTINUUM (Least Severe to Most Severe Concerns)

    1. Group guidance (guidance information for prevention & growth)

    2. Group counseling (counseling for prevention & remediation)

    3. Group psychotherapy (therapy for remediation)

III. GROUPS CLASSIFIED BY THEORETICAL ORIENTATION

    1. Gestalt counseling groups (based on the work of Frederick Perls)

    2. Transactional analytic groups (TA groups)

    3. Encounter groups (per self-theory and Carl Rogers)

    4. Adlerian groups (children, families, themes of belonging & inferiority)

    5. Psychoanalytic groups (also analytic groups/psychodynamic groups)

    6. Behavioral groups (short-range therapy based on learning theory; modeling, role
                playing, rehearsal, contracts, etc.)

    7. Rational-Emotive group therapy (also reality group therapy)

IV. GROUP MODELS FOR CHILDREN

    1. Play therapy (use of toys and play in order to focus on insight, verbalization
                of feelings, feedback, reducing anxiety)

    2. Story-Book counseling (story-telling with feedback)

    3. Puppet therapy (use of puppets to communicate to and with the child)

    4. Artistic groups (clay, painting, other media)

    5. Play group counseling (playroom activities for prevention and remediation)

V. GROUP MODELS BY LEADERSHIP STYLES

    1. Authoritarian group (power & destiny of the group rest with the leader)

    2. Democratic group (activities & process based on consensus of the group)

    3. Laissez-Faire group (little structure, direction, & leadership from the leader)

    4. Leaderless group (no assigned or defined leader; a leader arises or emerges)

VI. PROCESS-FOCUSED GROUPS

1. Marathon group (intensity of process, long length of meeting time)
2. Case-Centered group (focuses on individual members, one at a time)
3. Psychodrama group (role playing related to individual concerns)
4. Sociodrama group (role playing related to social concerns)
5. Sensory-Awareness group (focuses on internal & external awareness)
6. Activity-Interview group (recreational activity, to reduce tension, followed by discussion)
7. Confrontation group (frequent direct feedback & intense encounters to break down resistance and reluctant participation)
8. T-Group (honest feedback, self-disclosure, & observation-participation)

VII. CONTENT-FOCUSED GROUPS

1. Common-Problem group (all members have the same common problem)
2. Theme-Centered group (a predetermined group theme, e.g., women concerns, date rape, & concerns of the aged)
3. Synanon group (drug addiction; illicit drug use)
4. Alcoholics Anonymous (alcoholism)
5. Family therapy (focuses on family concerns, family dynamics, and individual family members)

VIII. TREATMENT-TRAINING GROUPS/ADJUNCTS TO COUNSELING

1. Relaxation therapy group (previously discussed in Section 6)
2. Meditation group (e.g., transcendental meditation and yoga exercises)
3. Exercise therapy group (e.g., jogging, aerobic exercises, & walking)
4. Biofeedback group (previously discussed in Section 6)
5. Bioenergetic group (body posturing, stretching, & positioning to reduce muscle tension)
6. Assertion training group (previously discussed in Section 6)
7. Values clarification group (exploration and clarification of values)
8. Attitudinal exploration group (sometimes called attitudinal reorientation)

IX. MISCELLANEOUS GROUPS/SPECIAL-PURPOSE GROUPS

1. Discharge group (discharge from a hospital or treatment setting)
2. Weight-Reducing group (per obesity)
3. Stop-Smoking group (e.g., Smokenders)
4. Cancer group (for patients of cancer or for patients and loved ones)
5. Peer-Facilitated group (or peer group counseling)
6. Consulting group (e.g., in mental health, family, professional, or school setting)
7. Study habits group
8. Couples group
9. Death-and-Dying group
10. Gay group
11. Women's group
12. Al-Anon (self-help group for spouses of alcoholics)
13. Al-Ateen (self-help group for teenagers with an alcoholic parent)

---

058   **CONSIDERATIONS IN STARTING A GROUP**

Questions to Raise in Considering Group Counseling

1. Will the type group considered meet the needs of prospective members?
2. Will anticipated benefits for prospective members outweigh possible disadvantages and cost (e.g., time of members/staff, cost of staff time, emotional energy invested, and risk of dropouts from group)?
3. Does participation in the group have the support of family, friends, and/or loved ones (e.g., spouse, parents, or very close friends)?
4. What type group should be established; or in what type group would a prospective member best benefit?
5. What type group, in terms of membership, will be cohesive and effective?
6. Should the group be an open group or closed group?
7. What should be the size of the group?
8. In what type setting should the group take place (where should it meet)?
9. How often should the group meet per frequency (e.g., once or twice a week)?
10. What should be the length of time per meeting (e.g., two hours)?
11. What should be the duration or life of the group (e.g., 10 weeks, 14 weeks, etc.)?

Other Considerations in Starting a Group

1. Client readiness
2. Similarity of prospective members (e.g., age, background, & educational level)
3. Counselor's like for and interest in the prospective members
4. Heterogeneous group (members with different problems) versus a homogeneous group (members with similar problems or same problem)
5. Method of screening and/or selecting members for the group
6. Ground rules for the group
7. Responsibility of each member to the group

Steps in Establishing a Group

1. Determine the needs of the clients or prospective members.
2. Assess the appropriateness of group counseling (based on Step 1).
3. Establish general goals for the group.
4. Identify and orient potential group members.
5. Select and prepare group members (via screening interview, assessment of expectations, and solicitation of a commitment to the group).
6. Develop and choose the group (composition by sex, length of meetings, frequency of meetings per week, & duration of group).
7. Hold the first meeting.

(For further reading related to this topic, consult Gazda, 1984; Ohlsen, Horne, & Lawe, 1988; and Yalom, 1985.)

References

Gazda, G.M. (1984). Group counseling: A developmental approach (3rd ed.). Boston: Allyn & Bacon.

Ohlsen, M.M., Horne, A.M., & Lawe, C.F. (1988). Group counseling (3rd ed.). New York: Holt, Rinehart & Winston.

Yalom, I.D. (1985). Theory and practice of group psychotherapy (3rd ed.). New York: Basic Books.

059   **GOALS AND OUTCOMES OF GROUP COUNSELING**

The following are considerations related to setting goals and defining outcomes for group counseling.

Criteria and Considerations for Setting Goals

1. What are the expressed goals of the client or prospective group member?

2. Are client goals unrealistic or unethical; and, if so, to what degree?

3. How are the goals related to the theoretical model or orientation of the group?

4. How are group goals related to the biases and orientation of the group leader(s)?

5. How do the goals for the group relate to the functioning setting of the client (e.g., job setting, educational setting, residential setting, and cultural setting)?

6. How should goal setting for the individual client coordinate with goal setting for the group? Moreover, what should be the role of the group member, the group, and the group leader(s) in setting goals?

7. How can goals for group counseling be translated into measurable and observable outcomes?

8. How will goal achievement and client outcomes be evaluated?

9. How do individual goals set for the client (or group member) relate to his or her basic needs as a human being?

10. What are possible barriers and risks involved in various goals for human change? (For example, how could involvement in a group and subsequent behavior change of a client affect his or her spouse and their relationship?)

General Goals for Group Counseling

1. The prevention and the remediation (or resolution) of client problems

2. Education about quality living

3. Information for insight and effective decision-making

4. Improved responsibility and rational thinking

5. Improved academic performance

6. Greater awareness of self and others

7. Improved interpersonal relations and social skills

8. Greater personal adjustment
9. Greater assertiveness and self-confidence
10. A healthy lifestyle
11. Greater understanding of oneself
12. The ability to cope with conflict and stress
13. Improved self-esteem

Outcomes of Group Counseling

The following are empirical outcomes of group counseling based upon research studies on groups (e.g., see reviews by Gazda, 1984; Ohlsen, Horne, & Lawe, 1988; and George & Dustin, 1988).

1. Increased self-concept measures
2. Increased self-actualization measures (e.g., on the POI - Personal Orientation Inventory)
3. Improved GPA (Grade Point Average)
4. Symptom reduction (via direct observation ratings or self-report inventories)
5. Improved interpersonal functioning (inside and outside the group)
6. Self-Acceptance, self-confidence, and self-reliance
7. Personality measures (improved scores)
8. Improved performance on academic achievement tests
9. Reduced state and trait anxiety (via anxiety inventories)
10. Decreased measures of aggression
11. Decreased incidents of depression

References

Gazda, G.M. (1984). Group counseling: A developmental approach (3rd ed.). Boston: Allyn & Bacon.

George, R.L., & Dustin, D. (1988). Group counseling: Theory and practice. Englewood Cliffs, NJ: Prentice-Hall.

Ohlsen, M.M., Horne, A.M., & Lawe, C.F. (1988). Group counseling (3rd ed.). New York: Holt, Rinehart & Winston.

060   THERAPEUTIC AND ANTITHERAPEUTIC FORCES IN GROUPS

Introduction

This topic includes therapeutic forces (forces that facilitate growth, therapy, and positive human change) in groups as well as antitherapeutic forces (forces that impede positive human change) in groups (see Ohlsen, Horne, & Lawe, 1988; Rogers, 1970; & Yalom, 1985).

Therapeutic Forces

1. Leadership (the group leader's/group leaders' motivation, support, facilitation, and positive modeling)

2. Expectations (the group members' understanding of and cooperation with the expectations of the group)

3. Client Readiness and Commitment (the client's readiness for group counseling; and a commitment to attend meetings, share experiences, help others, and change self)

4. Acceptance of Responsibility by Client and Counselor (i.e., responsibilities to the group and as related to their roles and agreed-upon expectations)

5. Attractiveness of the Group (the prestige of the group leader(s) and group members; the importance of perceived goals/theme; and the perceived ability of the group to meet the needs of its members)

6. Sense of Family/Belongingness (the group members' perceived sense of belonging and a sense of being a family of mutual support and care)

7. Communication, Feedback, and Sharing (understanding, information giving, focused listening, meaningful feedback, and self-disclosure)

8. Therapeutic Tension (normal anxiety and tension that are necessary in order to facilitate growth and human change)

9. Security (the group members' perceptions of the group atmosphere as secure and nonthreatening in regard to risk-taking, sharing, and providing feedback and participation in general)

10. Imitative Behavior/Modeling (the imitating of positive behaviors of group members or group leaders who serve as constructive role models)

11. Group Cohesiveness (a sense of developing closeness, support, and solidarity that contribute to therapeutic change)

12. Catharsis (an emotional release as well as a freeing up of feelings and tension)
13. Interpersonal and Social-Skills Development (developing empathy and insight,
                    learning appropriate responses, becoming less judgmental, and working
                    through transference)
14. Hope and Confidence (group members' faith and confidence in group counseling
                    and the group; and the group leader's/group leaders' faith in the
                    group members)
15. Universality and Identification (identifying with problems of group members; a
                    sense of commonality of problems as human beings or members of
                    a specific social group)

Antitherapeutic Forces

Antitherapeutic forces within groups can include (a) a member with a difficult
personality or behavior, (b) unethical or nonconstructive behavior by a group leader,
or (c) other conditions or events that can negatively affect the therapeutic atmosphere of the group or the welfare and growth of any of its members.

Examples follow:

1. The Grieving Member (a member who is preoccupied with a sense of loneliness,
                    helplessness, guilt about a loss—including the loss of a loved one in
                    death)
2. The Hostile Member (a member who feels rejected, hurt, and abandoned; who is
                    often aggressive, demanding, and even brutal; and who finds it diffi-
                    cult to accept the empathy of others)
3. The Anxious Member (a member who is predisposed by personality to be tense,
                    apprehensive, fearful of participation at times, easily hurt, and often
                    disorganized in thoughts).
4. The Depressed Member (the member who is frequently sad, energyless, tearful,
                    and hopeless)
5. The Monopolizing Member (a member who expresses the need to control the group
                    by holding its attention; one who constantly seeks recognition and who
                    tends to be self-centered)
6. The Silent Member (one who is withdrawn from the group process by not sharing
                    or providing feedback; tends to draw the suspicion and curiosity of
                    other members while foregoing meaningful growth by not participating)

7. The Socializer (The group member who wants everyone in the group to be his or her friend inside and outside the group setting; one who tends to socialize rather than function in a responsible, therapeutic role as member)

8. The Narcissistic Member (the selfish self-lover who loves the self to the exclusion and/or consumption of others)

9. The Jealous Co-Leader (the group leader who is overtly jealous of his or her fellow group co-leader; such behavior can result in open competition, conflict, and tension between the co-leaders that usually distract from effective therapeutic leadership and processing)

10. The Sexually Seductive Group Leader (the group leader who uses his or her status in the group to seduce sexually a group member, or who allows himself or herself to be seduced by a member--thus becoming involved in an unethical act that can have antitherapeutic and possibly legal consequences; also sexual overtones communicated between a group leader and member or between co-leaders to the distraction of the group process)

11. The Old-Pro Attitude of Experienced Members (experienced group members who tend to rival group leaders and/or who present the attitude to group members of "knowing it all")

12. The Intellectualizer (the group leader or group member who is preoccupied with what is right and wrong in terms of group behaviors and group events)

13. Violation of Confidentiality (serious suspicions or inadvertent revelations about violations of confidentiality by a group member or leader can influence adversely the entire therapeutic atmosphere of the group)

References

Ohlsen, M.M., Horne, A.M., & Lawe, C.F. (1988). Group counseling (3rd ed.). New York: Holt, Rinehart & Winston.

Rogers, C.R. (1970). Carl Rogers on encounter groups. New York: Harper & Row.

Yalom, I.D. (1985). Theory and practice of group psychotherapy (3rd ed.). New York: Basic Books.

061   TECHNIQUES AND EXERCISES FOR GROUPS

Introduction

This topic presents a variety of techniques and exercises appropriate for group work. They are organized into four categories by type and function: (a) verbal techniques, (b) nonverbal exercises, (c) role-playing exercises, and (d) miscellaneous techniques and exercises.

Verbal Techniques

- Information Giving. Verbally sharing meaningful and timely information.
- Confrontation. A nonthreatening means of directively encountering denied and resistive behavior.
- Interpretation. Inferring the meaning or cause of a group member's behavior.
- Reflection. Providing accurate feedback of feeling, mood, or content.
- Reassurance. Supporting and comforting a group member in a moment of difficulty, doubt, or emotional distress. (Also, see encouragement.)
- Questioning. Requesting information via a direct question or series of questions.
- Advice Giving. Recommending alternatives or options per possible courses of action.
- Summarizing. Pulling together or summing up the group session or a segment of what has transpired in the group session.
- Clarification. Requesting additional information, explanation, or rewording for the sake of clarity.

Nonverbal Exercises

- Touching Activities. Nonthreatening and non-sexual touch activities for the purpose of decreasing anxiety about touching and closeness, increasing awareness of self and others, and reducing resistive barriers.
- Eyeball-to-Eyeball Exercise. An activity involving two persons staring into each other's eyes without verbal exchange for about 30 seconds to two minutes. Afterwards, perceptions and feelings about the experience and what was communicated are shared.
- Body-Language Communication. The practice of communicating with body language as well as learning to read and analyze body-language messages.

- Facial Expressions. The practice of communicating and understanding different facial expressions that represent specific communicated messages.
- Trust Exercises. Exercises whereupon one member of the group tests his trust of another person or the entire group. For example, (a) one member falls backwards into the arms of a second group member who is entrusted to catch and protect the falling member, or (b) a group member stands in the center of a circle of standing group members and falls limply into the supportive hands of the protective circle that is entrusted to protect the encircled member from falling completely (sometimes the encircled person is pushed from member to member around the circle as he/she falls in different directions).

Role-Playing Exercises

- Role Reversal. In role playing, a group member plays a role that is opposite his or her natural behavior (e.g., a submissive person may play an assertive role). The member may also play the role of a real person or switch roles with another group member whose natural role is opposite in style.
- Behavioral Rehearsal. The use of role playing in order to practice and learn effective interpersonal skills or appropriate behaviors.
- Psychodrama. A role-played scene in the group setting for the purpose of assisting a group member or members to understand, clarify, or resolve a personal problem or concern.
- Sociodrama. A role-played scene or playlet employed to help members understand and clarify social influences on behavior; this exercise can also be used to teach socially appropriate behavior.
- Empty Chair. A role-playing exercise in which a group member role plays with an imaginary person in an empty chair (the group member sits opposite the empty chair and plays his or her role only or both roles). (This is a Gestalt therapy technique.)
- Monotherapy. A Gestalt therapy technique in which a group member writes a dramatic scene and role plays all characters (a means of facilitating awareness, playing out fantasies, and revealing repressed wishes and thoughts).

- Karpman Triangle. A technique of transactional analysis used in the group setting to assess games played between members in terms of three different roles: (a) the "persecutor," (b) the "rescuer," and (c) the
  "victim." After assessment of games, role playing may be employed
  in order to demonstrate the destructive games and in order to demonstrate "adult" or appropriate ways of relating.

Miscellaneous Techniques/Exercises

- Fishbowl Technique. A technique that provides for a smaller, functioning group
  encircled by a larger, observing group (a circle within a circle). The
  inner group encounters and processes while the outer group provides
  meaningful feedback at junctions or afterwards. Participants and observers are allowed to switch roles individually, therefore, allowing
  freedom to function as participant or observer as the need arises.
- Homework. Designated tasks or activities for the group or group members to
  carry out between group meetings.
- Hot Seat. A Gestalt group technique whereby the group leader focuses intense-
  ly on one member of the group at a time, with the member usually
  sitting opposite the dialoguing group leader. There is sometimes
  intermittent input from other group members.
- Modeling. The use of live models within the group setting or the use of
  vicarious models via film, verbal illustration, or other media, i.e., for
  the purpose of shaping appropriate behavior through imitation learning.
  In behavior group therapy, the model is frequently reinforced in order
  to enhance or diminish his or her value to influence other group members.
- Feedback. The sharing of verbal as well as nonverbal reactions about a group
  member to that group member directly. The feedback is honest and
  therapeutically facilitative.
- Sharing Hunches. A technique of Gestalt therapy whereupon group members are
  encouraged to share their initial feelings or perceptions of other
  members and their problems in the form of "hunches" (e.g., "It is my
  hunch that you...").

- Sociometry. A technique for measuring or assessing interpersonal preferences among members of a group based upon a predetermined criterion (e.g., "Who do you like the best and second best in the group?"). The sociogram (a related concept) is the diagram that represents the results of sociometry.

(For some of the descriptions presented under this topic of "group techniques and exercises" as well as other related information, see the glossary in Glanz & Hayes' (1967) Groups in Guidance, Harper's (1981) Dictionary of Counseling Techniques and Terms, and Jacobs, Harvill, & Masson's (1988) discussions of group skills (Chapter 5) and group exercises (Chapter 9) in their Group Counseling: Strategies and Skills.)

References

Glanz, E.C., & Hayes, R.W. (1967). Groups in guidance (2nd ed.). Boston: Allyn & Bacon.

Harper, F.D. (1981). Dictionary of counseling techniques and terms. Alexandria, VA: Douglass.

Jacobs, E.E., Harvill, R.L., & Masson, R.L. (1988). Group counseling: Strategies and skills. Monterey, CA: Brooks/Cole.

Notes

SECTION 8

Special Topics

062   **CONSULTING IN COUNSELING**

Definitions of Consulting

- A triangular relationship involving (a) a consultant, (b) a consultee, and (c) a system or client (a unit or person that is indirectly helped) for the purpose of improving the skills, knowledge, and effectiveness of the consultee.

- A helping process by which a resource person (the consultant) improves or facilitates the effectiveness of a consultee and/or organized unit.

Roles of the Consultant

- Can function in the role of expert, resource person, trainer, provider of direct services, change agent, collaborator, specialist, negotiator, or evaluator.

- Is a nonjudgmental, nonauthority, and noncompetitive figure.

- Does not attempt to counsel the consultee during the consulting relationship.

- Can function as a paid or nonpaid professional, as a person inside or from outside a system, and as a counselor-consultant (a counselor functioning as a consultant, e.g., with colleagues as a trainer or resource person).

- Usually, focuses on a unit external to the consulting relationship or external to the consultee (e.g., a staff problem, an evaluation task, or a single counseling case).

- Has implications in terms of (a) the role of the elementary school counselor as consultant, (b) the role of the counselor as a professional consultant, and (c) the role of consultation in mental health and higher educational settings.

Steps in the Consulting Process

1. <u>Pre-Entry</u> (the consultant evaluates his or her skills and beliefs in terms of assessing whether a job or role is appropriate)

2. <u>Entry</u> (the consultant defines and establishes the consulting relationship and role; establishes a written agreement or contract if appropriate)

3. <u>Gathering Information</u> (obtains all possible information in order to assess and clarify a presenting problem)

4. <u>Defining the Problem</u> (assesses and determines goals for change)

5. <u>Determining a Possible Solution</u> (analyzes and synthesizes information in seeking the best solution to the stated problem and goals)

6. <u>Stating Objectives</u> (stating desired outcomes that can be accomplished and measured within the designated time of work and under the conditions of the setting)

7. <u>Implementing the Plan</u> (implementing or carrying out the intervention/consulting based on the stated objectives of Stage 6)

8. <u>Evaluation</u> (monitoring activities and measuring final outcomes)

9. <u>Termination and Follow-Up</u> (discontinue the consulting contact; follow up intermittently or at a later date if necessary)

(These steps or stages can be varied, to a degree, or abbreviated according to the nature of the consulting task and arrangement. See Kurpius, 1978; Kurpius and Robinson, 1978; and Conoley and Conoley, 1982.)

Theories of Consultation

GENERAL THEORY OF CONSULTATION (Blake & Mouton, 1978)

- Behavioral and group patterns are cyclical (repeated from day to day).
- The consultant needs to intervene to break nonproductive cycles.
- Three dimensions of consultation include (a) types of intervention, (b) focal points, and (c) identity of the client.
- Types of intervention are (a) acceptant (assuring), (b) catalytic (assisting), (c) confrontation (challenging), (d) prescription (prescribing things to do), and (e) offering theories and principles for solving the problem.

CAPLANIAN MODEL (Caplan, 1970)

- The focus is on mental health consulting.
- The two types of consultation are (a) case-centered (consulting about a case/client) and (b) consultee-centered (consulting to improve a staff or a consultee's skills/knowledge).
- The consultant avoids a therapeutic role, direct confrontation, bias, supervision, and education; however, does interpret the biases and themes of the staff.
- The consultant focuses on themes or representations of unresolved problems; and seeks to minimize or eliminate these themes and representations.

INTEGRATED THEORY (Kurpius, 1978)

- The process of consultation is triadic (consultant, consultee, & client/system).
- Consulting modalities are (a) the provision mode (providing services), (b) the prescription mode (exploring alternatives), (c) the collaborative mode (facilitating solutions), and (d) the mediation mode (an insider resolving a problem with fellow colleagues).
- The stages of consulting are (a) pre-entry, (b) entry, (c) gathering information, (d) defining the problem, (e) determining a solution, (f) stating the objectives, (g) implementing the plan, (h) evaluating progress, and (i) termination.

BEHAVIORAL CONSULTATION (Russell, 1978)

- The focus is on social learning principles, especially antecedents and consequences of the behaviors of both the consultee and client.
- The five steps of behavioral consultation are (a) observation (observing the behaviors of the consultee and the client), (b) functional analysis (analyzing the causes of behavior), (c) objective setting (i.e., for intervention), (d) behavioral intervention (via behavior therapy techniques), and (e) withdrawal of intervention.

Applications of Consultation

The following are examples of consultation in the areas of mental health and education as related to counseling and student development concerns:

1. Elementary school counselors consulting with parents about special needs and problems of their youth.
2. Elementary school counselors consulting with teachers and administrators concerning curricular development, social problems of the school, and program development.

3.   Counseling psychologists providing direct testing and diagnostic services to the staff of school counselors or staff of a community mental health center.
4.   Counseling psychologists consulting with college and university personnel about concerns of and related to students such as health and drugs, race relations, social adjustment, crime and safety, and financial needs.
5.   Counseling psychologists consulting with industry, corporations, and organizations on concerns of human effectiveness/efficiency, organizational development, behavioral systems, and improving work performance and satisfaction.
6.   Counselors and counseling psychologists providing information and/or skills at professional meetings or to professional staff in the form of papers presented or training sessions (or a combination of both).
7.   External experts or resource persons consulting with a counselor or a group of staff on a difficult counseling case or on a topic of therapeutic concern.
8.   Counseling psychologists consulting with judicial staff, the courts, or lawyers on legal cases or issues.
9.   Counselors providing prevention consultation to youth and adults on popular areas of concern including alcohol and drugs, loss and grief, date rape, AIDS/venereal diseases, and child sexual abuse.
10. Consultation with divorcing couples per negotiation and mediation.

(The above examples are a limited listing of possibilities for consultation by counselors and as related to the professional field of counseling. For further readings on this topic, see a recent special issue devoted entirely to "consultation"--i.e., The Counseling Psychologist, Volume 13, Number 3, July 1985, pages 333-527. Also see two special issues of the Journal of Counseling & Development, February and March, 1978, Volume 56, Numbers 6 and 7, pages 320-448.)

References

Blake, R.R., & Mouton, J.S. (1978). Toward a general theory of consultation. Journal of Counseling & Development, 56, 328-330.

Caplan, G. (1970). The theory and practice of mental health consultation. New York: Basic Books.

Conoley, J.C., & Conoley, C.W. (1982). School consultation: A guide to practice and training. New York: Pergamon.

Kurpius, D. (1978). Consultation theory and process: An integrated model. Journal of Counseling & Development, 56, 335-338.

Kurpius, D., & Robinson, S.E. (1978). An overview of consultation. Journal of Counseling & Development, 56, 321–323.

Russell, M.L. (1978). Behavioral consultation: Theory and process. Journal of Counseling & Development, 56, 346–350.

063   SUPERVISION OF COUNSELING

Definition

Supervision of counseling is a one-to-one relationship whereby a more experienced counselor or psychotherapist facilitates the professional development of the counseling skills and competence in a less experienced counselor or counselor-in-training. (That is, the more experienced counselor being the supervisor and the less experienced counselor being the supervisee.)

Other Characteristics of Supervision

- The supervisor-supervisee relationship involves the supervision of a counselor who is usually simultaneously counseling a client. The content of supervisory discussion revolves mainly around the counselor's (supervisee's) counseling performance in reference to the counseling case.

- The supervisor is ethically responsible in the relationship for the professional growth of the counselor as well as indirectly for the welfare of the client.

- The supervisor usually does not come into contact with the counselor's client except through knowledge from tape-recorded dialogue, counselor notes/discussions, and case records.

- The growth of the counselor is encouraged and monitored in a stage-to-stage manner. The supervisor's feedback is tentative when possible and provides both positive and negative observations, however, in a constructive way.

- The supervisor-supervisee relationship has ethical and legal implications in regards to the supervisor's relationship to and responsibility for the counselor as well as an indirect responsibility for the welfare of the client.

Criteria for the Supervision of Counselors

1. Quality and tone of the counselor–client relationship (rapport/conditions of effective counseling displayed)

2. Professional responsibility and ethical awareness

3. An understanding of the dynamics of the client's problem and the dynamics of the counseling relationship

4. Resourcefulness and creativity of the counselor in solving the client's problem

5. Ability to accurately identify verbal counseling techniques employed

6. Adequate development of goals and objectives for counseling; and the choice of intervention/theories for achieving these goals and objectives

7. Whether the counselor self-evaluates his or her counseling performance from time to time

8. Counselor's skills in process movement (e.g., opening and closing the session, summarizing material at strategic points, and terminating the counseling relationship)

9. Counselor's practice and ability per writing case reports and documenting material and circumstances related to counseling cases

Questions for the Supervisor's Self-Evaluation

1. Do I provide constructive feedback and encouragement to the supervised counselor? Is my feedback tentative versus absolute?

2. Do I discuss cooperatively the goals of counseling and intervention for each case with the supervisee?

3. Do I supervise around a preestablished set of criteria that are related to the counselor's growth and skills? (For example, such as the criteria listed in the section above.)

4. Am I aware to emphasize the importance of helping the client?

5. Am I conscious of legal and ethical issues as related to my role as supervisor as well as the counselor's role in counseling the client? Do I consider whether a case might be too complicated for the beginning or less-experienced counselor?

6. Do I consider and employ supervisory methods such as audiotape/videotape reviews, analysis of tapescripts, observation (one-way mirror), and co-counseling? Is my final evaluation of the supervisee in written form?

Ethical and Legal Considerations

In general, the supervisor must take every caution and responsibility possible for the professional growth of the supervisee and the welfare/rights of the client. The following are just a few concepts and principles related to ethical and legal concerns in the supervision of counselors:

Due Process. Refers to the counselor's (supervisee's) right to be "forewarned" or knowledgeable of training objectives, assessment procedures, and evaluation criteria; also has reference to procedural rights of the supervisee in training or a beginning counselor who may be under probation for the initial contract period.

Dual Relationship. The supervisor must avoid the establishment of two kinds of relationships with the supervisee, such as both a supervisory professional relationship simultaneously with a sexual relationship. This same phenomenon should be avoided between the supervisee (or counselor) and his/her clients.

Informed Consent. The supervisor should make sure that the counselor informs the client (and/or parents for minors) of all aspects of counseling, especially informing and acquiring consent for observation and taping during the counseling session.

Vicarious Liability. The supervisor is legally responsible for wrongful acts of the supervisee. Therefore, the supervisor should take precautions in terms of supervising a counselor closely and frequently, not assigning the counselor to a case that is too difficult per the counselor's level of competence, and making sure the counselor follows ethical and legal guidelines in his or her relationship to each counseling case.

Confidentiality. The supervisor and the counselor should respect the confidentiality of each client along with the client's right of privacy; however, should make the client aware of the limits of confidentiality if he or she presents a threat to another person or society (in reference to the counselor's "duty to warn" another or society of possible danger).

(For background reading for this topic, see Hess, 1980; Whiteley, 1982; and Bartlett, Goodyear, & Bradley, 1983. For readings on ethical and legal aspects of supervision, see Cormier & Bernard, 1982; and Hummel, Talbutt, & Alexander, 1985.)

References

Bartlett, W.E., Goodyear, R.K., & Bradley, F.O. (Eds.). (1983). Supervision in counseling II (Special issue). The Counseling Psychologist, 11 (1).

Cormier, L., & Bernard, J.M. (1982). Ethical and legal responsibilities of clinical supervisors. Journal of Counseling & Development, 60, 486-491.

Hess, A.K. (1980). Psychotherapy supervision: Theory, research & practice. New York: John Wiley & Sons.

Hummel, D.L., Talbutt, L.C., & Alexander, M.D. (1985). Law & ethics in counseling. New York: Van Nostrand Reinhold.

Whiteley, J.M. (Ed.). (1982). Supervision in counseling I (Special issue). The Counseling Psychologist, 10 (1).

064   EVALUATION AND COUNSELING

Evaluation Defined

- Evaluation is the comparison of an object of interest against a standard of acceptability.

- Evaluation is a process for assessing effectiveness in terms of stated goals and objectives as compared to actual outcomes and performance.

- Program evaluation is a method of providing meaningful information to decision-makers about program effectiveness in order to aid in resource allocation and to assist in process changes.

  (See Wheeler & Loesch, 1981; and Anderson, Ball, Murphy, & Associates, 1975.)

Nature of Evaluation

1. Evaluation can be viewed as different from research by some and as a special form of research by others. Some even see it as overlapping with research.

2. Evaluation of a counseling program is primarily concerned with testing its effectiveness in achieving stated goals and objectives (i.e., goals and objectives of the program as a whole).

3. Evaluation of counseling, itself, involves assessing the effectiveness of achieving goals and objectives set for each client—often in terms of behavior outcomes and human changes that are observable and measurable.

4. Evaluation is <u>more likely</u> to employ soft data and soft design versus that of traditional empirical research. For example, program evaluation may use client files, program records, self-report inventories, interview data, and direct-observation data. Moreover, there could be questions about the validity of such data and the circumstances under which the data were collected.

5. Evaluation is <u>more likely</u> to use both qualitative and quantitative data as compared to traditonal research methods, and is <u>less likely</u> to be rigorous in regards to research controls and procedures.

Needs and Purposes of Evaluation

1. In general, as a means of information for decision-making and improvement.

2. As a requirement for a grant or funded project related to counseling.

3. As required for a counseling unit of a school, university, or community program for planning in general and for budgetary considerations.

4. As a self-evaluation of counseling for personal and professional improvement and accountability.

5. As a means of information for decisions about personnel (as related to supervisory feedback, job maintenance, job promotion, and nonrenewal of contract).

6. In assessing the effectiveness of counselor training and continuing education (e.g., counseling courses, workshops, and conference sessions).

7. In the evaluation of treatment effectiveness (e.g., alcoholism treatment, obesity treatment, illicit-drug-addiction treatment, and anxiety treatment).

8. As a method of assessing prevention programs and social education projects (e.g., drug/alcohol education, sexuality education, preventive health, and marriage and family living).

Foci of Evaluation

1. <u>Needs Assessment</u> (appraising needs and priorities for services, information, resource allotment, or program development)

2. <u>Materials Evaluation</u> (evaluating the appropriateness of effectiveness of, and need for counseling-related materials)

3. <u>Staff Evaluation</u>   (assessing the effectiveness of staff, e.g., counseling staff, support staff, and administrative personnel)

4. <u>Accreditation Self-Study</u>   (evaluating a counseling center or counselor education program against external criteria set forth by an accrediting body, e.g., the American Association for Counseling and Development or the American Psychological Association)

5. <u>Training Evaluation</u>   (assessing the effectiveness of training as related to counseling; i.e., including the effectiveness in accomplishing training goals, covering content, teaching skills, functioning of trainer(s), and the appropriateness of instructional media and materials)

6. <u>Contract Performance Evaluation</u>   (evaluating the quality and quantity of performance against designated duties and tasks written in a legal contract)

Evaluation Designs

1. <u>Ex Post Facto Design</u>   (an evaluation study carried out "after the fact" and based upon available records from the past)

2. <u>True Experimental Design</u>   (An evaluation that plans for controls, randomization, pretest-posttest measures, and manipulated treatment in order to effect outcomes or changes)

3. <u>Quasi-Experimental Design</u>   (an experiment that <u>lacks control</u> over who gets treatment and when, or that lacks a control group or opportunity for randomizing the assignment of treatment)

4. <u>Longitudinal Evaluation</u>   (a long-term monitoring of a counseling program's effectiveness as an example; usually involves repeated observations and measurements of criteria over a period of years; could also focus on a long-term evaluation of selected clients who are followed up after treatment)

5. <u>Historical Evaluation</u>   (evaluated effectiveness based on the historical events, performance, and records of a long-existing program (or phenomenon); historical evaluations examine effectiveness according to past events and records while longitudinal evaluations plan to examine effectiveness based on data collected over a period of years in the future)

6. Survey (assessing the status of a single entity or group of entities; e.g., an eval-
    uative survey of "problems and concerns of students at a particular
    school" or a survey of "the uses and purposes of all publicly funded
    mental health centers in a given city")

Issues in Evaluation

1. The question of how the results should be used versus the lack of use of the
    results.

2. The anxiety and perceived threat of evaluation as related to personnel and pro-
    gram survival; to what degree are these feelings/perceptions real versus imagined?

3. The increased use and sometimes overuse of evaluation; is this movement practical
    and justified, or is it an exaggerated precaution related to legal concerns—mainly
    concerning possible law suits or making a case for personnel decisions?

4. The issue of employing possibly invalid or unreliable data from faulty evaluation
    in order to make important decisions about program budgets and personnel.

5. The question of consensus, measurability, and operational definitions as related to
    goals of counseling.

6. The issue of confidentiality and privacy of data related to staff evaluations (e.g.,
    the evaluation of counseling staff and counselor education faculty).

7. The problem of human bias in evaluation, especially when direct observers, judges,
    and supervisor ratings are employed (e.g., bias related to sex, race, cultural style,
    age, or even theoretical orientation).

References

Anderson, S.B., Ball, S., Murphy, R.T., & Associates (1975). Encyclopedia of educational
    evaluation. San Francisco: Jossey-Bass.
Wheeler, P.T., & Loesch, L. (1981). Program evaluation and counseling: Yesterday,
    today, and tomorrow. Journal of Counseling & Development, 59, 573-577.

065 **WORKSHOP TRAINING**

Introduction

The following outline provides limited, practical guidelines for planning a counseling workshop (or a workshop in general):

PLANNING THE WORKSHOP
- Selecting a theme (useful, timely, & feasible)
- Selecting a city or site (convenience to audience, attractiveness, & availability of local facilities)
- Deciding the length or duration of the workshop (e.g., 1 to 3 days)
- Considering overall cost (training rooms, speakers, coffee & tea, materials, advertisements, & the question of who will pay for participant food/lodging— participants usually arrange for meals and hotel rooms with assistance of the workshop planners)
- Dividing labor for planning and carrying out the workshop
- Selecting competent speakers/trainers (cost, telephone confirmations, letters of agreement exchanged or contract, & travel/lodging arrangements—also ground transportation from airport to workshop site if appropriate)
- Determining deadline(s) for registration and manner of accepting payment
- Assessing and estimating total cost (consider the length of workshop, materials, facilities, paid staff, speakers/trainers' fees & expenses, rental of equipment, advertisement, etc.)

ADVERTISING THE WORKSHOP (Plan Far Ahead for Announcing)
- Brochures (design, printing, & mailing)
- Journal and/or magazine ads (can be very expensive)
- Newspapers and professional newsletters (may need camera-ready copy of ad according to type and amount of space)
- Radio & television public announcements (inquire about free time or public service announcements)
- Word of mouth (use key individuals for telephone networking and personal contacts)
- Memoranda and business letters (mailed with brochures or separately to key personnel)

DEVELOPING MATERIALS FOR THE WORKSHOP
- Roster of workshop registrants (by name, address, phone)
- A program or schedule of workshop activities and presentations
- Free educational pamphlets related to the topic of the workshop
- Booklets, manuals, reference materials, and packages
- Materials/articles for sale and exhibit
- Audio/visual material (slides, film, video, transparencies, posters, etc.)
- Program certificates for participants (as proof of attendance/registration)
- Name tags
- Pencil and pads
- Receipt book or forms (if necessary, for on-site registration)

WORKSHOP ROOMS, ATMOSPHERE, FURNITURE, & EQUIPMENT
- Adequate room size(s) with desk arrangement or table-chair arrangement, especially if much writing is anticipated
- Blackboard or flip chart for illustrations
- Pointer (for illustrations)
- Audio-Visual equipment if necessary (check hotel resources or local rentals)
- Lectern with microphone (and/or a panel arrangement)
- Water for speakers
- Coffee, tea, etc. for breaks, i.e., for participants as well as trainers

REGISTRATION FOR THE WORKSHOP
- Pre-Registration versus on-site registration (both recommended; checks for pre-registration should be mailed ahead of time to clear and on-site registration may consider cash or equivalent only—or risk bad checks for services delivered)
- Registration table set up with packets and name tags (plus typewriter or other equipment for on-site registration, receipts, etc.)

WORKSHOP MANAGEMENT & LOGISTICS
- Starting the workshop and sessions on time (only vary schedule if absolutely necessary, feasible, and agreeable with participants)
- Acquiring background information for introducing speakers (predesignate the person who will introduce each speaker)
- Establishing mechanisms for process evaluation and outcome evaluation

- Allowing for adjustments and developing needs (for the unexpected or crises)
- Arranging for security services if deemed necessary (safety of participants, cash on hand from registration, and expensive equipment or items)
- Arranging for eating (provide information about nearby acceptable restaurants and/or consider building one or more lunch/dinner activities into the workshop—e.g., luncheons or banquets)
- Collaborate closely with designated persons from the hotel staff (or workshop facility staff, if not using a hotel) about occurring needs during the workshop
- Wrap up the workshop at the closing session (administer any questionnaire or inventory necessary for the evaluation of the workshop)

FOLLOW-UP
- Close out final, on-site business matters (hotel, speakers, & any participants)
- Mail thank-you notes and letters immediately following the workshop (e.g., the following day or week)
- Pay unpaid bills as soon as possible and close any unfinished business
- Consider and possibly carry out a follow-up evaluation (in addition to the evaluation data collected at the workshop); a telephone follow-up of representative participants may be adequate for feedback reflecting afterthoughts or further thoughts on the effectiveness and usefulness of the workshop.

066   PROPOSAL WRITING

A proposal is a well-written and well-outlined idea for a project that simultaneously requests funding, some type of approval, and/or joint cooperation. Almost all proposals submitted to federal agencies and private foundations include a budget and a request for funding. Some agencies and foundations request competitive proposals on a topic, concern, or work task. This announcement of request is called a Request for Proposal or RFP. Below is an outline of content that is usually included in a proposal.

DEFINE THE PROBLEM AND PROJECT
- What is the basic nature and purpose of the project?
- How serious is the need for such a project?
- Are the problem and purpose stated in specific terms?

GIVE THE BACKGROUND OF THE PROBLEM
- What set of educational, social, economic, and/or political realities are involved as related to the problem?
- Why is the problem or topic appropriate for funding by the agency or foundation to which it is presented?
- Why is the proposing person or organization capable of addressing the problem?
- Are research studies and data presented in order to justify the immediacy of the problem and the need to address the concern?

IDENTIFY NEEDS THE PROJECT SEEKS TO MEET
- Are the needs stated in clear, concise, and specific terms?
- Is there documentation or data showing how needs for the project were assessed?
- Do the needs identified in the proposed project correspond with the funding concerns and priorities of the funding resource?

PRESENT THE GOALS AND OBJECTIVES
- Do goals and objectives derive from and correspond with the general purpose of the proposed project?
- Do the goals and objectives correspond with the needs derived from the needs assessment for the project?
- Are the objectives stated in operational and measurable terms; and can the objectives be subjected to successful evaluation?

PREPARE A CALENDAR OF ACTIVITIES/EVENTS BASED ON THE OBJECTIVES
- Can the project be completed in the time allocated in the proposal and/or funding period?
- Is the timetable or schedule realistic given tasks to be completed and possible social, political, and human barriers or setbacks?
- Are the activities, events, and tasks of the timetable clearly stated and described?
- Do the activities have a clear and coordinated relationship to the proposed objectives?
- Is there linkage of various stages of the project in terms of the overall purpose and objectives?
- Are there alternatives or backup mechanisms in the case an activity or task in the timetable is held up significantly or cannot be completed as proposed?

DESCRIBE PROJECT PARTICIPANTS
- What is the target population? Or, what group of participants will be serviced, trained, studied, or involved as recipients of the project's activities?
- What will be the criteria and procedures for selecting and recruiting the participants?
- Will enough qualified, prospective participants be available to complete the project as proposed?
- How will the proposed project be presented to the community or university of its origin, especially to the specific population(s) to be served?

IDENTIFY SUPPORTIVE GROUPS, SYSTEMS, AND PERSONS
- What community agencies, organizations, institutions, and leaders will be involved with the planning and execution/support of the project?
- What physical facilities and resources will be provided in support of the project and its activities?
- What services, volunteers, and professionals will be available as supportive resources?
- Describe any proposed community or university advisory group for the project; what would be the function of the group and who will make up its membership?

DEVELOP AN EVALUATION DESIGN
- Will the design include procedures for evaluation of the process?
- What aspects of the evaluation design will provide for the assessment of the project's outcomes and effectiveness as related to its purpose and objectives?
- Who will perform the evaluation; and how will it be carried out from start to finish? Will the evaluation be carried out by project staff or will outside consultants be hired to carry out the evaluation?

SHOW HOW THE PROJECT WILL BE MANAGED/STAFFED
- What staff will be needed for the project?
- What are the job descriptions and roles of the different staff positions?
- How will the staff be recruited and placed (indicate methods and the timetable for hiring)?
- What staff members will be responsible for what activities, tasks, and events?
- What will be the man-hour time required for the duration of the project? What will be the breakdown of staff positions by time?

- What are the qualifications and competencies of the proposed staff (describe and include copies or summaries of the prospective staff members' vitae or résumés)?

PROPOSED BUDGET

The proposal may include budgetary allowances for direct costs as well as indirect costs. Direct costs include itemized expenses paid via payroll (staff) or vouchers/purchase-order methods. Indirect costs include general expenses necessary for the operation of the project or grant; expenses encumbered by a university or agency housing the grant (such as financial services in managing the grant, energy costs to the physical plant, and space used for activities). Indirect cost is usually calculated as a percentage of the grant or the direct costs.

Some Examples of Budgetary Items

SALARIES AND WAGES

Consultants
Research assistants
Interviewers
Secretary
Typists
Research subjects
Staff benefits
Program director
Instructional personnel (trainers)
Statistician/computer programmer
Hourly wages

EQUIPMENT/FURNITURE

Fixed equipment
Movable equipment
Office equipment
Office furniture
Equipment rental
Furniture rental
Equipment installation
Micro-Computer(s)
Computer printers & other hardware

MATERIALS AND SUPPLIES

Office supplies
Test materials
Duplicating supplies
Computer supplies
Typewriter supplies
Questionnaires/inventories

TRAVEL

Administrative travel
Professional travel (conferences, etc.)
Field work
Consultants' travel
Automobile rental

SERVICES

Photographic processing
Computer time/processing
Copying or duplicating
Printing services
Other services/service contracts
Telephone & communications

OTHER COSTS

Space rental (if additional space needed)
Subscriptions to periodicals/books
Tuition and fees (professional meetings)
Computer software/programs
Counseling information kits
Audio-Visual resources

067   COUNSELING NON-WHITE ETHNICITIES

Introduction

For the purposes of this topic, non-white ethnicities have reference to Black Americans, American Indians, and Hispanic Americans.

Similarities

1. The majority of Blacks, Indians, and Hispanic Americans tend to be among the lower income groups.

2. Geographically and socially, all three ethnic groups tend to be isolated from mainstream America; e.g., Blacks in the urban ghetto, Indians on the reservation, and Hispanics in the barrio.

3. All three ethnic minority groups are visibly non-white; therefore, they have been racially discriminated against as groups in terms of educational, economic, social, and political opportunities. (Hispanics tend to see themselves as non-Anglo.)

4. External controls over the lives and destinies of non-white ethnicities have, to a great degree, created and perpetuated a common feeling of powerlessness, fatalism, and self-blame.

5. The education of youth among all three ethnic groups very often indicate a high school drop-out rate and problems of academic achievement and social adjustment.

6. The three American ethnic groups are either legally defined or culturally defined according to law or place of birth and rearing. Therefore, law and culture very often take precedence over genetic or anatomical racial attributes. For example, one who looks white physically, can be classified as a Black American if it is established that one parent is Black. Another example is that a person of mixed parentage (e.g., Black and Indian) who is born and raised on an Indian reservation can be defined as an Indian—even though the person may look much more Black in genetic attributes than Indian. Moreover, a Black person from Puerto Rico can be classified as Hispanic and is very likely to identify more with Puerto Rican or Latin Americans than with Black Americans (primarily due to language and cultural similarities).

7. The cultural values of the three ethnic groups are less likely to differ and conflict among themselves than they are likely to differ from and conflict with values of White, middle America.

Differences

1. The three non-white ethnicities differ in <u>population sizes</u> with Blacks having the largest U.S. population among the three, followed by Hispanics and then American Indians. (The Hispanic population is rapidly increasing, plus there remains the question of undocumented Hispanics who cross the border and reside illegally.)

2. There are often <u>language differences</u>. Blacks usually use English only as the language of communication, while Hispanic or Spanish-speaking Americans are often bilingual--many preferring Spanish over an ability to speak English to some degree. Indians may speak English and, to a degree, different tribal languages according to tribal membership and background.

3. Ethnic minorities frequently differ in religious preference and practice. Black Americans tend to be Protestant (mainly Baptist) and Hispanic Americans tend to prefer Catholicism. Numerous Indians practice their own adopted form of Christianity mainly through the Native American Church, while others often practice some form of traditional tribal religion.

Behavioral and Cultural Styles

<u>BLACKS</u>
- Tend to use body language and imaginative language.
- Often value White, middle-class, American values.
- Are likely to experience self-blame, feelings of powerlessness, and perceptions of external control.
- Black middle class and working professionals are likely to have high self-concepts while Black lower class groups often score low on self-esteem/self-concept measures.
- Have traditionally studied (in college) the social sciences, the arts, and education with a recently increasing interest in business administration (<u>lack of study</u> in the physical sciences, applied mathematics, banking, marketing, engineering, and the professions of medicine and law).

<u>AMERICAN INDIANS</u>
- Tend to value advice and wisdom.
- Believe that God is one and a part of all things.
- Often have a respect for bravery, individual freedom, and silent observation.

- Value self-fulfillment, acceptance of others (without condition), and self-acceptance; also value sharing with others versus competition with others.

- Believe that all things are sacred and related (a oneness and connectedness).

HISPANIC AMERICANS
- Tend to value machismo (manly courage and duty).
- Have a great respect for and obedience to a Supreme Being or God (i.e., as Roman Catholics).
- Tend not to favor intellectualism or the joining of formal organizations.
- Are oriented to the present more than the future.
- Frequently view the world from a fatalistic point of view.
- Take great pride in their culture, family, heritage, and religion.
- Tend to respect authority figures.

Counseling Needs of Non-White Americans
HEALTH NEEDS
- **Blacks** have a need for health care and services, especially as related to a high incidence of hypertension, strokes, heart/cardiovascular disease, alcoholism, drug addiction, AIDS, sickle cell disease, and certain cancers.

- **Indians** have a need for health care and services related to a high prevalence of alcoholism, trachoma (infectious eye disease), cirrhosis of the liver, alcohol-related accidents, heart disease, and numerous infectious diseases.

- **Hispanics** have a need for health care and services, primarily as related to a high incidence of tuberculosis, influenza, cardiovascular diseases, infant mortality, and injuries from automobile accidents.

EDUCATIONAL NEEDS
- Need for preschool experiences for children of the three ethnic groups.
- Need for curricular courses and materials that reflect the culture and the history of the three ethnic groups; also quality schools, materials, and teachers.
- Need to address the problem of school drop-outs per preventive and follow-up programs and efforts.
- Need for college preparatory programs as well as supportive programs at colleges and universities (also greater activities in recruitment and retention of minorities).

VOCATIONAL/CAREER NEEDS

- Accessibility to successful social models of one's own ethnic group who can provide inspiration for career decision-making.

- Knowledge about the world of work and its required preparation and training.

- Basic minimal educational skills (computing, reading, writing, speaking, etc.) necessary for effective job functioning and advancement.

- Marketable job skills via school training or special vocational training.

- Personal, social, and human relations skills in working effectively with others in the job setting.

- Greater opportunity for professional training in higher education (especially in the career areas of the applied sciences, the physical sciences, health and medicine, law, business, engineering, and applied mathematics).

PSYCHOLOGICAL NEEDS

- Fulfillment of psychological needs related to a positive self-image, personal confidence, physical/psychological adequacy, sense of control over one's destiny, and appreciation for ethnic culture and heritage.

- Proper attention, acceptance, love, nurturance, and experiences for minority babies and children during the critical years of development.

- Positive reinforcement and straightforward feedback/encouragement on the part of counselors, teachers, and significant leaders of minority communities.

- Self-Improvement, community improvement, and economic improvement for the purpose of personal and racial pride and esteem.

- Opportunities for personal achievement and successes in a number of different areas of endeavor in order to improve self-esteem and self-concept.

EXPERIENCES

- Travel beyond one's own ethnic neighborhood to other communities, cities, states, and countries.

- Experiences in the reading of periodicals and books both in the home and library settings.

- Exposure to television programs that enhance learning and knowledge such as children's educational programs, news, essays, documentaries, and cultural presentations.

- Exposure to training and experiences that can positively influence language skills.

- Participation in programs and activities related to one's ethnic heritage as well as the heritage and cultures of other ethnic groups.

Techniques of Counseling

BLACKS

1. Develop empathy with and understanding of Black Americans.
2. Make frequent and primary use of cognitive and action-oriented counseling techniques.
3. Employ group counseling techniques and approaches where possible.
4. Support the development of reading, writing, and calculating skills or, in general, basic educational and functional skills (especially applicable to preschool, elementary school, and adult education).
5. Consult with persons who are in a position to help the Black client; for example, parents, teachers, school administrators, university personnel, religious leaders, community leaders, job supervisors, and health personnel.
6. Encourage abled and potentially capable Black youth to take a college preparatory curriculum at the school level.
7. Seek financial support for Black families of poverty and for Black college students in need.
8. Develop job skills in and job opportunities for Blacks, as well as assisting Black clientele in taking advantage of job training/openings.
9. Use outreach counseling in order to identify and gain access to Black clients in need of help.
10. Understand the popular rhetoric and language of Black culture, especially Blacks of your catchment population or caseload.
11. Counsel Black clients into careers where they are underrepresented.
12. Develop an orientation for working closely with the Black client's family and community in regards to the presenting problem.
13. Seek to observe and understand culturally oriented body language.
14. Use and interpret tests results with caution and with consideration for the cultural background and social class of the Black client.

For documentation and further explanation of counseling techniques with Black Americans, see Atkinson and Morten's (1983) book on Counseling American Minorities, Harper and Bruce's (1984) discussion of "counseling strategies for Black survival," Vontress' (1971) view of "aggressive counseling" with Blacks, McDavis' (1978) eclectic model, Gunnings and Simpkins' (1972) "systemic counseling," Harper & Stone's (1974; 1986) "transcendent counseling," Smith's (1973) "action-oriented counseling" with Black youth, and McFadden's (1986) "stylistic dimensions" of counseling.

AMERICAN INDIANS

1. Know and appreciate the behavior, values, and cultural way of the Indian.
2. Listen attentively and provide alternative solutions or recommendations when appropriate and timely. In other words, feel free to use advice giving, however, present alternatives or a number of options instead of a single course of action recommended.
3. Develop, at least, a minimal understanding and use of Indian language and tribal terms or concepts.
4. Deal with the silence of the Indian slowly, trustfully, and without pressure.
5. Employ and interpret results of tests with caution, understanding how the values, culture, and motives of the Indian way can conflict with the Western content and purposes of tests/test-taking.
6. Use outreach techniques in identifying and helping the Indian American, since there could be reticence about approaching a counselor.
7. Treat the Indian client as a friend, be available for helping, be patient with change, and remain open-minded.
8. In vocational counseling and career counseling, be cognizant of how Indian values and beliefs might conflict with the Western world of work. For example, (a) a job encouraging extreme competition and overemphasis on profits can conflict with Indian values for sharing, (b) a job involving the widespread harvest of trees for lumber or destruction of forestry for commercial development can conflict with Indian beliefs in the conservation of resources and the sacredness of life, and (c) a job emphasizing personal possessions and status may conflict with Indian values for intrinsic appreciation.
(See Bryde, 1971; Atkinson & Morten, 1983; and Spang, 1971.)

HISPANIC AMERICANS

1. Understand the culture and the heritage of the Spanish-speaking person.

2. Develop and improve skills in the Spanish language.

3. Facilitate ways in which the client can fulfill any expressed religious needs as related to a strong Hispanic preference for Catholicism.

4. Encourage experiences outside the Hispanic community that will improve skills in the use of English along with increasing a greater understanding and appreciation of the larger outside world.

5. Work closely with community workers and parents of Hispanic school youth, especially in the case of Puerto Rican parents and youth.

6. Use group guidance in sharing information about careers and about the rich cultural heritage of Hispanics.

7. Employ group counseling over individual counseling where and when possible. (Of course, individual counseling may be necessary and more appropriate in a situation of crisis, a request for information, or problems of emotional conflict that may require individual attention.)

8. Be aware of the underrepresentation of Hispanics in the job market, job training programs, and higher education, along with addressing these needs through career counseling and educational counseling.

(See DeBlassie, 1976; Atkinson & Morten, 1983; & Pollack & Menacker, 1971.)

References

Atkinson, D.R., & Morten, G. (1983). Counseling American minorities: A cross-cultural perspective (2nd ed.). Dubuque, IA: Wm. C. Brown.

Bryde, J. (1971). Indian students and guidance: Minority groups and guidance (Guidance Monograph Series, No. VI). Boston: Houghton Mifflin.

DeBlassie, R. (1976). Counseling with Mexican-American youth: Preconceptions and processes. Austin, TX: Learning Concepts.

Gunnings, T., & Simpkins, G. (1972). A systemic approach to counseling disadvantaged youth. Journal of Multicultural Counseling & Development (formerly, Journal of Non-White Concerns in Personnel & Guidance), 1, 4-8.

Harper, F.D., & Bruce, G.C. (1984). Counseling strategies for Black survival. NAPW Journal, 1, 11-18.

Harper, F.D., & Stone, W.O. (1974). Toward a theory of transcendent counseling with Blacks. Journal of Multicultural Counseling & Development, 2, 191-196.

Harper, F.D., & Stone, W.O. (1986). Transcendent counseling: A multimodal model for Multicultural counseling. International Journal for the Advancement of Counselling, 9, 251-263.

McDavis, R.J. (1978). Counseling Black clients effectively: The eclectic approach. Journal of Multicultural Counseling & Development, 7, 41-47.

McFadden, J. (1986). Stylistic dimensions of counseling minorities. International Journal for the Advancement of Counselling, 9, 209-219.

Pollack, E., & Menacker, J. (1971). Spanish-Speaking students and guidance: Minority groups and guidance (Guidance Monograph Series, No. VI). Boston: Houghton Mifflin.

Smith, E.J. (1973). Counseling the culturally different Black youth. Columbus, OH: Charles E. Merrill.

Spang, A. (1971). Understanding the Indian. Journal of Counseling & Development, 50, 97-108.

Vontress, C.E. (1971). Counseling Negroes: Minority groups and guidance (Guidance Monograph Series, No. VI). Boston: Houghton Mifflin.

068   **ALCOHOL AND DRUG COUNSELING**

Nature of Alcohol

- Drinking alcohol is a drug that affects the brain and thus changes the psycho-active mood of the person.

- Drinking alcohol is scientifically referred to as ethanol or ethyl alcohol.

- Alcoholism is a disease characterized by heavy and compulsive drinking of alcohol which is associated with family problems, job problems, chronic physical illnesses, accidents, and interpersonal conflict. Alcoholism can also be defined as an addiction to the drug alcohol.

Alcohol and the Human Body

- Alcohol is not digested, but rather absorbed through the walls of the digestive tract and into the blood stream whereupon it is transported to the liver, brain, and other organs/tissue of the body.

- The liver is primarily responsible for metabolizing or breaking down alcohol into its byproduct or derivatives which are eventually eliminated from the body by urination, perspiration, and/or exhalation.

- The greater the amount of alcohol in the blood stream, the greater the impact on the brain; and, consequentially, the greater the influence on human behavior (e.g, body control, slurred speech, unsteadiness, coordination, and poor sleep--all influenced by centers of the brain).

- Too much alcohol ingested at once (such as in drinking contests) can cause death; and heavy drinking over many years can lead to brain damage and a number of associated illnesses and diseases.

Alcohol-Related Disorders/Illnesses
- Liver disease (e.g., cirrhosis, fatty liver, & hepatitis)
- Neurological disorders & brain damage
- Cancer of the esophagus (or esophageal carcinoma)
- Stomach ulcers, diarrhea, and other digestive disorders/illnesses
- Metabolic disorders (e.g., hypoglycemia and hyperglycemia)
- Nutritional deficiences (especially vitamin C and the B vitamins)
- Disorders and illnesses of the skin, pancreas, & cardiovascular system
- Fetal alcohol syndrome (a syndrome in newborns of alcoholic women, characterized by mental retardation and facial disfiguration)

Social Consequences of Alcoholism/Alcohol Misuse
- Alcohol-Related vehicular accidents
- Accidents (home, industrial, and recreational)
- Financial problems and/or bankruptcy
- Job problems, interpersonal problems, and family disruption
- Violence and homicide (while under the influence as victim or perpetrator)
- Various alcohol-related crimes including robbery, rape, assault, spousal abuse, & child abuse

Treatment & Counseling (Alcoholism/Problem Drinking)
GOALS OF ALCOHOLISM TREATMENT
- Sobriety
- Physical rehabilitation and health
- Employment and/or career adjustment (in some cases)
- Social adjustment/effective family living
- Psychological adequacy & independence

TREATMENT MODALITIES

- Medical treatment (for related symptoms/illnesses)
- Detoxification
- Individual and group counseling
- Alcohol education
- Alcoholics Anonymous
- Al-Anon & Al-Ateen (for family members with an alcoholic)
- Halfway House Living (for transition from treatment to community living)
- Family therapy
- Vocational counseling (job placement, readjustment, training, etc.)

COUNSELING STRATEGIES

- Outreach counseling
- Referral counseling (to and from programs/agencies)
- Behavior therapy
- Cognitive/rational therapies
- Job placement/vocational counseling
- Family counseling
- Consultation (with community agencies, family, police/courts, social services, etc.)
- Follow-Up (after inpatient treatment and/or termination of counseling)

Illicit Drugs/Chemical Substances

COMMONLY USED DRUGS

- Tobacco (contains nicotine which stimulates the heart and central nervous system)
- Alcohol (calming effect; stimulates mildly & then depresses the central nervous system)
- Marijuana (stimulates; induces relaxation, risk-taking, & a sense of well-being; can enhance sensory perception)

STIMULANTS (stimulate nervous system; cause euphoria & high mood; & can result in irritability and overactivity)

- Caffeine (in coffee, tea, cola drinks, & chocolate—mildly lifts mood)
- Amphetamines (diet pills including dexedrine & benzadrine; can cause yo-yo effect)
- Cocaine (includes snow, crack, & freebase rock; can bring about increased energy, alertness, & euphoria)

DEPRESSANTS (Downers, depress the nervous system, include tranquilizers and sedatives)

- Valium & Librium (mild tranquilizers frequently prescribed for anxiety and irritability)
- Barbiturates (very dangerous & addictive; can result in side effects of confusion, loss of memory, dizziness, and convulsions; can be very dangerous when taken with alcohol)

NARCOTICS (derived from opium or its derivatives; also can be created via synthetic methods)

- Heroin (one of the most popular of the narcotics or opiates; can create a sense of euphoria while relieving pain; can also cause drowsiness and stupor)
- Other Narcotics (morphine, methadone, demerol, & codeine)

HALLUCINOGENS (stimulate & depress; change visual & auditory perceptions; can cause hallucinations)

- LSD (causes disorientation; small amount can be potent; in clear, colorless, liquid form, sometimes served on sugar cubes, tablets, or blotter paper for licking)
- PCP (usually in a liquid or powder form, angel dust; can be taken orally, injected, or sprayed on cigarettes or marijuana for smoking; along with crack, is one of the most dangerous substances; can cause a number of effects including numbness)
- Mescaline (a derivative of the peyote cactus; can be sliced and chewed)

INHALENTS (substances or chemicals inhaled for their psychoactive effects)

- Include gas fumes, hair sprays, deodorants, glues, paint thinners, & fingernail-polish removers among others

Drug Treatment & Counseling

GOALS OF TREATMENT

- Drug-Free state
- Stable and/or meaningful employment
- Drug and health awareness
- Improved interpersonal relations
- Improved social adjustment
- Improved overall health

TREATMENT MODALITIES
- Drug detoxification
- Methadone maintenance (use of the drug methadone under medical supervision in order to reduce the dependence on heroin; also see other drug maintenance programs)
- Medical/physical rehabilitation
- Drug education/drug prevention
- Self-Help support groups (for loved ones & relatives of drug addicts)
- Group psychotherapy/group counseling
- Self-Regulation training (e.g., biofeedback, relaxation, & meditation)

COUNSELING STRATEGIES
- Behavior therapy
- Cognitive therapies
- Individual counseling/therapy
- Synanon groups (drug groups involving confrontation & the breaking down of defenses & resistance)
- Assertion training (primarily, for learning to say no to drug-using peers)
- Verbal confrontation (in both individual and group counseling)

(For references related to the topic of "alcohol and drugs," see Tobias, 1986; Dusek & Girdano, 1987; & Hafen with Brog, 1983.)

References

Dusek, D.E., & Girdano, D.A. (1987). Drugs: A factual account (4th ed.). New York: Random House.

Hafen, B.Q., with Brog, M.J. (1983). Alcohol (2nd ed.). St. Paul, MN: West Publishing.

Tobias, J.M. (1986). Kids & Drugs: A handbook for parents & professionals. Annandale, VA: Panda Press.

---

069   **COMPUTERS AND COUNSELING**

Computer Defined

A computer is an electronic device that can record, manipulate (including calculate), store, and analyze alphabetical and numerical data. A computer can also control other machinery and devices through programmed instructions.

Specific Functions of a Computer

It is believed by some that a computer can do anything that it can be programmed to do. Below are selected popular functions of today's computers, including personal computers or micro-computers:

1. Keeping and managing files (e.g., of items, cases, & accounts)
2. Managing mailing lists
3. Performing calculations (e.g., in mathematical & statistical analyses)
4. Teaching and instruction (via instructional programs)
5. Storing data for future update, retrieval, and processing
6. Managing an inventory (such as in sales items in stock or with office materials)
7. Communicating with other computers (or other persons with computer access)
8. Entertaining (e.g., computer games & musical programs)
9. Word processing
10. Desktop publishing (typesetting and designing camera-ready copies for printing, including newsletters, reports, & books)
11. Solving problems (through programs with logical statements for serial decision-making and/or decision-making based on given conditions)
12. Drawing design (e.g., as for creative art, engineering designs, & architectural designs)
13. Simulating theoretical models

Computer Programming

Computer programs are developed from computer languages, which are different symbolic means of talking to or instructing a computer in order to get it to perform specific tasks. Languages are used to develop the many sophisticated software programs used today. The following are common languages used to develop computer programs:

- BASIC (Beginner's All-Purpose Symbolic Instruction Code)
- COBOL (Common Business Oriented Language)
- FORTRAN (FORmula TRANslator—for algebraic problems & notations)
- Assembly Language (a language used with an assembler to convert symbolic statements into machine language—or the language of the computer being used)
- Other computer languages include Snobol, ALGOL, Pascal, & PL/1

Computer Concepts

- Hardware (the computer and its peripheral equipment)
- Software (the computer programs & programming/software aids)
- Memory (refers to the storage capacity of a computer or computer peripheral; usually measured in terms of "bytes"; e.g., 1 byte = a character, digit, or part of a word; K = 1000 bytes & a megabyte = 1 million bytes)
- Laser Printer (a computer printer capable of printing in high definition or at the highest quality of printing sharpness)
- RAM (random-access memory)
- ROM (read-only memory)
- Mouse (a finger- and hand-controlled device for moving a pointer or "cursor" on the monitor of the computer for the purpose of easy editing of text and commands to the computer)
- Hypercard (a personal-information tool kit for personalized office use, recently pioneered by Apple Computer, Inc.; a software program for office/personal use)
- Modem (a device that enables computers to communicate over circuit lines of telephones)

Computer Uses in Counseling

1. The use of the computer to administer, score, and/or report tests and inventories of clients (e.g., software programs for the Strong Interest Inventory and the Self-Directed Search). Also, see software programs available from companies such as the Consulting Psychologists Press and the Psychological Corporation.

2. The use of the IBM-PC and Apple Computers to assist in the interpretation of test scores and the printing of results and profiles, e.g., as with the WISC-R and the WAIS-R.

3. The employment of computers to assist in the rapid and efficient retrieval of client-specific career and educational information on a monitor or screen as well as the print-out of such information for the client's future reference and use.

4. The use of computers or computer terminals to access university data on clients or mental health data on patients.

5. The use of computers in research and evaluation for the purposes of statistical analysis, the construction of figures and tables for presenting data/analyses, and the word

processing of the report. For example, for statistical analysis, see SPSS^X and SPSS/PC (1986) and SAS (1979).

6. The use of computers or computer terminals for literature searches and literature reviews (e.g., the American Psychological Association's PsycLIT).

7. The use of computers in the management of client cases, caseloads, client scheduling, and other information, records, and processes (be cautious about highly sensitive, confidential, and private information as related to the possibility of inappropriate access and use of computer files).

8. The use of computers in the education of counselors, the inservice training of helping professionals/staff, and the computer-assisted education of clients.

(For directories of software and computer-based products for counseling and psychology, see Krug, 1988; and Stoloff & Couch, 1988.)

References

Krug, S.E. (1988). Psychware sourcebook, 1988-1989. Kansas City, MO: Test Corporation of America.

SAS (1979). SAS: Statistical Analysis System user's guide. Raleigh, NC: SAS Institute.

SPSS (1986). SPSS^X: User's guide (2nd ed.). Chicago: SPSS, Inc.

Stoloff, M.L., & Couch, J.V. (1988). Computer use in psychology: A directory of software. Washington, D.C.: American Psychological Association.

070   **ETHICS AND LEGALITIES IN COUNSELING**

Introduction

Laws and statutes can differ by state and ethical standards can differ across professional associations; however, there are numerous laws and ethical considerations with common themes. Below is a listing of some of these, keeping in mind that counselors should consult, know, and observe the laws of the state in which they practice and the ethical standards of their primary professional association:

1. Competence. A counselor or helping professional should only provide psychological services based upon his/her training and professional experience.

2. <u>Responsibility</u>. Counselors, other helping professionals, and counselor educators must be responsible for their actions and the consequences of their actions in relationship to those (clients, students, supervisees, & research subjects) with whom they work.

3. <u>Confidentiality</u>. There should be every effort to protect the privacy of the client and information shared in the counseling relationship, except where law requires otherwise or wherein the client may pose a threat to the public or another person (per the principle of "duty to warn").

4. <u>Testing & Assessment</u>. There should be proper use of testing/assessment instruments and their results. The counselor should be cognizant of the security of tests as well as the rights of the client or testee, including the right to know his/her test results and how they will be used.

5. <u>Public Statements</u>. In making statements to the public (e.g., via television, radio, newspaper, and announcement of counseling services), the counselor should be accurate, objective, responsible, and tentative if necessary. The counselor should weigh seriously his or her qualifications to discuss a particularly topic in public before doing so.

6. <u>Research & Human Subjects</u>. The researcher of counseling should observe ethical and legal principles related to research involving human subjects and as related to the dignity and welfare of human subjects.

7. <u>Professional Practice</u>. The counselor should seek to improve professional practices, his/her professional growth, and ethical behaviors of colleagues. Also, the counselor or helping professional should seek sound and effective relationships with associates, agencies, professional associations, and clients.

8. <u>Consultation/Supervision</u>. In the consulting and supervisory relationships, counselors, counselor educators, and other helping professionals should maintain the same level of professional responsibility, competence, confidentiality and rapport as in the counseling relationship. The consultant and the supervisor should be aware of legal responsibilities along with their ethical and professional responsibilities.

9. Moral/Legal Standards. The counselor or helping professional should adhere to the moral and legal expectations of the community or state in which he or she practices. There should also be care to avoid a dual relationship with a client, supervisee, or student (e.g., having both a professional counseling relationship and a sexual relationship with a client).

For further readings on "ethics and legalities in counseling," see American Psychological Association (1981); Corey, Corey, & Callahan (1988); and Hummel, Talbutt, & Alexander (1985).

References

American Psychological Association (1981). Ethical principles of psychologists. American Psychologist, 36, 633-638.

Corey, G., Corey, M.S., & Callahan, P. (1988). Issues and ethics in the helping professions (3rd ed.). Pacific Grove, CA: Brooks/Cole.
(See Appendices, pages 385-430, for ethical standards for the American Association for Counseling & Development, the American Psychological Association, and other professional associations.)

Hummel, D.L., Talbutt, L.C., & Alexander, M.D. (1985). Law and ethics in counseling. New York: Van Nostrand Reinhold.

Notes

(Counseling Techniques)*

Abreaction. In psychoanalysis, a technique which facilitates the client's calling to awareness painful experiences or material that have been repressed. It is employed as a means of emotional release.

Acceptance. A verbal technique that expresses the counselor's interest in and understanding of what the client is communicating. Examples are "um-huh" and "yes."

Activity-Interview Group Counseling. A group approach involving an activity (a game or sport for physical release of tension and rapport building) followed by group counseling (group dialogue and discussion).

Adjuncts to Psychotherapy. Therapeutic training or activities that are employed as supportive or complimentary adjuncts to psychotherapy; adjuncts such as biofeedback and relaxation training.

Advice Giving. A verbal counseling technique which cautiously provides advice, alternatives, or options for the client's consideration.

Aftercare. Ongoing treatment or counseling in the community or home setting for the purpose of helping the client to adjust after a period of inpatient or hospital care; any follow-up services after release from counseling or treatment.

Aggressive Counseling. An approach by Clemmont Vontress for counseling with Black youth; employs directive counseling techniques, outreach counseling, motivation, personal assistance, and follow-up.

Ahistoric Therapy. Therapy that does not focus on the past experiences or history of the client but rather on here-and-now behaviors.

Al-Anon. A group approach for the treatment and support of family members of alcoholics; also an organization with the same purpose.

Al-Ateen. A group approach developed to help and support teenagers of alcoholic parents.

Alcoholics Anonymous (AA). A group approach for the treatment of alcoholics; an international organization of alcoholics with local group chapters.

---

*Reprinted from: Harper, F.D. (1981). *Dictionary of counseling techniques & terms*. Alexandria, VA: Douglass.

Alternative Interpretation. A form of interpretation in which the counselor provides an alternative interpretation to the one that the client makes about his or her own concern or behavior; the counselor's alternative interpretation is offered to provide realistic meaning and therapeutic inferences for the client.

Anecdotal Records (or Reports). Nonjudgmental descriptions of a client's behavior in a given situation which are recorded narratively by an observing counselor or some other professional observer.

Approval. Often used in behavior therapy, a verbal technique that expresses the counselor's agreement with a client's behavior in order to influence the recurrence or maintenance of the behavior.

Art Therapy. The use of artistic media and expression as an outlet or therapeutic activity.

Assertion Training. Refers to training a person to express repressed feelings toward another person, usually feelings expressing opposition or a negative reply to a request.

Attentiveness. Refers to the counselor's total attention to and involvement in the client's concern during the counseling process; requires intensive listening and observing by the counselor.

Attitudinal Reorientation. Refers to a technique involving the identification, analysis, and reorientation of attitudes with the goal of changing unhealthy attitudes; associated with Frederick Thorne.

Autobiography. a self-report counseling technique used to obtain information about the client's views and feelings in relationship to his or her own life; a brief self-written report of one's life for counseling purposes in general.

Aversive Therapy. A learning theory or behavior therapy technique in which an aversive stimulus is presented concomitantly with an inappropriate or unwanted response in order to inhibit the occurrence of the response (differs from punishment where the aversive stimulus occurs after the inappropriate behavior).

Behavioral Rehearsal. A technique of using repetition or practice in order for the client to learn effective interpersonal skills or appropriate behaviors.

Behavior Therapy. Any counseling therapy that is generally based on the principles of learning and conditioning; sometimes referred to as learning theory, behavioral therapy, or behavior modification.

Bibliotherapy. The use of recommended readings or literature, including books, to facilitate therapeutic change.

Bioenergetics. A therapeutic approach that employs stretching specific muscle groups and learning effective breathing techniques in order to reduce tension and depression.

Biofeedback. A technique of training persons to control or change autonomic responses once thought to be involuntary. The mechanism of change is not understood; however, the principles are believed to be associated with learning theory.

Biography of an Ideal. a technique to acquire themes that suggest a client's ideals, ambitions, and goals; the client constructs information on a model person who has influenced his/her life and writes a brief biography.

Brief Psychotherapy. Short-Term psychotherapy of several weeks to several months with a focus on the resolution of present problems via setting up direct or concrete goals.

Carbon Dioxide-Oxygen Inhalation. A technique of inhaling a specific gas to reduce anxiety; associated with Wolpe's reciprocal inhibition (also called "carbon dioxide-oxygen therapy").

Case Conference. A conference on one client or case attended by counseling staff members and/or specialists for the purpose of presenting, reviewing, and analyzing all possible information about the case.

Case History. A listing of information collected on one client; the information or data cover a number of years of the client's life.

Case Study. An intensive study of one client involving a summary and analysis of all available data concerning the problem or issue.

Catharsis. A talking-out experience in counseling or psychotherapy by the client for the purpose of releasing tension or repressed feelings.

Chemotherapy. The use of drugs in the treatment of psychopathology or personality disorders such as schizophrenia, hyperactivity, and epilepsy; in general, the use of drugs in the progressive treatment of disease or dis order.

Choice Awareness. An approach to counseling which focuses on helping the client to understand behavior and to make better choices in life; it was influenced by concepts of transactional analysis; however, is more appropriate for use with children and adolescents.

Client-Centered Therapy. A counseling theory developed by Carl R. Rogers; focuses on feelings, self, and experiences; employs reflection as its major counseling technique; client-centered therapy as opposed to counselor-centered therapy. (This theory is also referred to as person-centered therapy.)

Closed Question. A question asked by the counselor that either limits the client to a specific answer or a yes-or-no answer.

Cognitive Therapy. A counseling or therapy approach that focuses on thinking or mental processes in modifying behavior; often involves training, skills development, thought control, and other cognitive-oriented processes and techniques.

Common Problem Group. A counseling group in which all clients or members in the group have the same common problem or concern.

Computer-Assisted Counseling. Refers to the use of programmed computers for the retrieval of guidance information as an aid to the client's decision-making process.

Confrontation. A verbal counseling technique which is highly directive; used to encounter denied or unconscioulsy motivated behaviors; also a technique of Gestalt therapy which points out discrepancies in behavior and makes the client aware of what he or she is doing at the moment. Confrontation facilitates realistic behavior and the control of specific drives.

Conjoint Family Therapy. Refers to simultaneous counseling with the client and members of the client's family.

Contract. A verbal or written agreement between the counselor and the client as a technique for facilitating the achievement of a therapeutic goal. It provides structure, motivation, incentive for commitment, and assigned tasks for the client to carry out between counseling sessions.

Counterconditioning. In behavior therapy, a technique whereby a new conditioned response is associated with an incompatible conditioned response for the purpose of eliminating it.

Couples Counseling. Refers to counseling two persons together or separately in regards to problems in their relationship; usually deals with heterosexual couples or relationships.

Covert Modeling. A technique whereby the client is encouraged to imagine a model performing a role in which he or she would like to perform in a real life situation. Clients often create imaginary scenes that accompany the imagined model and anticipate themselves acting in the role of the model.

Covert Rehearsal. Refers to the individual's learning of new information or new behavior through private repetition of the information or behavior.

Dance Therapy. Dance exercises or routines for therapeutic expression, reduction of tension, and/or loss of body weight; in general, the use of dance for therapeutic outcomes.

De-Reflection. In logotherapy, a technique which assists the client to ignore anticipated anxiety by diverting his or her attention to something else.

Diagnosis. A step in counseling and psychotherapy which usually involves the collection, collation, analysis, and interpretation of data on the client for the purpose of identifying and understanding problems or concerns; also the third step in Williamson's directive counseling.

Diagnostic Interview. an interview designed to ascertain information for the diagnosis and prognosis of a client's problem.

Doubling. A technique whereby a group member provides feedback to another member by first imitating (through role playing) the undersirable behavior of the member and secondly role playing appropriate behavior that the member should display in a given life situation; the group member who provides role playing feedback usually sits adjacent to the member with the presenting problem.

Drug Therapy. The treatment of behavior disorders (e.g., hyperactivity, epilepsy, depression, and extreme tension) with appropriate medical drugs.

Eclectic Counseling. A theory of counseling that selects techniques or features from existing counseling theories and systematically applies them to the particular problem of the client; associated with Frederick Thorne.

Electrical Stimulation. A very mild and harmless electric shock administered to inhibit an inappropriate response.

Emotional Flooding. A technique in learning theory involving the client's high level of exposure to a real anxiety-provoking stimulus (such as a phobic object) in order to facilitate overcoming the irrational fear; associated with Wolpe's theory of reciprocal inhibition.

Empathy. A personality condition of effective counseling; the counselor's ability to "feel with" or "feel into" the client's frame of reference.

Empty Chair (Empty Seat). In Gestalt therapy, a role-playing technique employing a client and an imaginal person in the empty chair. The client sits opposite the empty chair when speaking to the imaginal person; a technique in which the client plays his/her role and the role of an imaginal person or partner.

Encouragement. A verbal counseling technique which expresses support or the client in an ongoing or anticipated endeavor.

Essay. A technique whereby the client is requested to write on a selected theme for the purpose of revealing therapeutic information.

Exercise Therapy. The systematic use of physical exercise for therapeutic purposes.

Family Therapy. The treatment of two or more family members simultaneously or as a group; can involve one or more therapists.

Feedback. The counselor's sharing of honest, facilitative reactions and opinions with the client about that client's behavior or verbal comments.

Fight Training Exercises. Simulated verbal and physical fighting under therapeutic supervision for the purpose of resolving interpersonal conflict or stimulating assertiveness.

Filial Psychotherapy. Role playing in which parents learn to function as psychotherapists and play therapists with their children.

Fishbowl Technique. In growth groups, a technique that divides the group into two subgroups whereby one group (the outside group) observes and provides feedback on the dynamics of the inside group. The two groups usually form a circle within a circle and observers and participants are often allowed to switch roles.

Follow-Up. In general, refers to methods of following clients who have left counseling, a treatment program, or a school; also a service of a guidance program. Follow-Up assists clients with new and old problems.

Free Association. In psychoanalysis, a technique which facilitates the client's spontaneous verbal expression of any thoughts or feelings that come to mind; especially repressed material or feelings.

Functional Analysis. In behavior therapy, the identification and examination of environmental stimuli that cause specific responses and behaviors.

Here-and-Now. In growth groups primarily, a focus on what is happening at the moment in helping the client to become aware of inner feelings as well as relationships with others; often associated with T-Groups, Gestalt therapy, and encounter groups.

Homework. Refers to activities assigned for the client to carry out between counseling sessions such as trying out new behaviors, imitating behavior, or reading therapeutic literature.

Hot Seat. In Gestalt group therapy, a technique of intensively focusing on one member of the group at a time; the member sits opposite the group leader and dialogues on a life problem with intermittent input from other members upon request by the leader.

Hypnosis. A technique used in psychotherapy; a therapeutically induced trance-like or sleep-like state of altered consciousness in which the hypnotized person is highly susceptible to suggestibility, instructions, and recollection of forgotten events. This technique was formerly called "mesmerism."

Ignoring. In behavior therapy, a technique of ignoring or not rewarding (by not acknowledging) an inappropriate response for the purpose of decreasing and eventually eliminating the occurrence of that response.

Impersonal Illustration. A verbal technique in which the counselor shares an experience of an anonymous person in order to make a therapeutic point or offer a solution (also, see personal illustration).

Implosive Therapy. A technique that is similar to emotional flooding; however, it presents simulated fear situations (as opposed to real ones) for the purpose of helping the client to overcome anxiety-provoking stimuli. Sometimes, the simulated fear stimuli have pscyhoanalytic meaning for the client.

Incomplete Thought. A verbal technique whereby the counselor pauses during a sentence in order to allow the client to complete the sentence.

Information Giving. A verbal technique for sharing meaningful and timely information with the client during the counseling session.

Intake Interview. A screening or diagnostic interview often used with prospective clients who are about to enter counseling or treatment.

Interpretation. A verbal technique in counseling and psychotherapy wherein the meaning or cause of the client's behavior is inferred and understanding is communicated; associated with psychoanalytic theory, existential psychotherapy, and Rotter's social learning approach.

Involvement. In reality therapy, a technique or disposition of the counselor characterized by authenticity, openness, friendliness, and nonanalytical straightforwardness.

Jogotherapy. A treatment-training approach that systematically applies jogging programs to specific human problems. It programs jogging speed, distance, environmental setting, and time of day to the needs of the client; the use of jogging for therapeutic purposes.

Johari Window (or Johari Awareness Model). A model of awareness in interpersonal relations that represents various behaviors about the individual that may be known and unknown to self and others. This model or technique is frequently used in group counseling or growth groups in general.

Karpman Triangle. A technique of transactional analysis that is used to assess games; the triangle represents three roles that game-playing persons employ: (a) the "persecutor" (one who feels he/she is better than others), (b) the "rescuer" one who thinks he/she knows more than anyone else), and (c) the "victim" (one who plays a helpless role). The Karpman Triangle may be used in groups to identify the specific game-playing role of each member and to show relationships among game-playing persons in the group.

Marathon Group. Refers to an intensive, continuous sensitivity group session that lasts from 12 to 72 hours and allows for short breaks; is often held on weekends.

Masterful Inactivity. A technique in eclectic counseling employed to delay client action by use of explanation and justification for inactivity at the moment; it facilitates the postponement of action until a later or more appropriate time.

Meditation. Mental and sometimes physical exercises for the purpose of producing relaxation, improved thought processes, and insight into oneself and the world; includes transcendental meditation, zen meditation, and various yoga methods.

Megavitamin Therapy. The use of large doses of vitamins to treat or control disease/disorders; a form or aspect of orthomolecular therapy.

Microcounseling. A method of training counselors through the use of videotaped feedback.

Milieu Therapy. Refers to an approach which emphasizes meeting the client's needs via the development of a therapeutic setting, atmosphere, or environment. The therapeutic environment or milieu can be a treatment setting (including staff attitudes and physical setting) as well as the client's natural environments (family, school, etc.).

Milling Around. The initial stage in an encounter group in which members engage in superficial talk and exploration as a sign of resistance to opening up to new persons and to a new process of relating.

Monotherapy. In Gestalt therapy, a technique in which the counselor requests the client to write or create a dramatic scene and role play all characters involved; the client is encouraged to role play personal fantasies or repressed wishes for the purpose of facilitating awareness and therapeutic discussion.

Multiple Counseling. Counseling in which two counselors counsel one client or in which one counselor counsels two clients; it usually involves three individuals and takes place in the counselor's office.

Music Therapy. The systematic and applied use of music in therapy, especially in mood modification or changes in psychological state.

No Excuses. In reality therapy, has reference to the counselor not entertaining or accepting excuses for contracted behavior that is not carried out or for irresponsible behavior in general.

Nonsexist Counseling. Refers to an area of counseling which assists both females and males to become aware of sex-role stereotyping as well as to learn to redefine their roles as men and women or girls and boys.

Opening Techniques. Refer to techniques used by the counselor in the very beginning or the counseling relationship for the purpose of establishing rapport and trust.

Outreach Counseling. Refers to the counselor's going outside the traditional counseling office or setting in order to counsel clients in their own natural setting.

Paradoxical Intention. A technique of logotherapy used in assisting the client to confront anticipated anxiety. Sometimes a relieving type of humor is employed to help the client assuage anxious thought and thus prepare for an anxiety-provoking situation.

Parent Discussion Groups. Discussion groups that involve expectant parents or parents with children of the same age group.

Passive Listening. Refers to intensive and attentive listening by the counselor in order to allow a client to express hostility, anxiety, or other forms of resistance; a patient form of listening which assists the client in dissipating antitherapeutic feelings or attitudes.

Peer Counseling. Refers to peers in a group counseling situation who help and support each other; also has reference to persons of the same age group who counsel their fellow age-mates or each other, especially adolescents; associated with B. Varenhorst.

Personal Illustration. A verbal technique whereby the counselor uses an example of his or her own experience for the purpose of making a therapeutic point or alluding to a solution for the client's problem.

Persuasion. A directive, verbal technique of counseling aimed at altering irrational thought or irresponsible behavior.

Photocounseling. A technique that uses still photos about the client's lie in order to obtain insight into the client's behavior and needs and in order to facilitate rapport, communication, and behavior change.

Placebo Therapy. Refers to the use of a placebo, which has no intrinsic therapeutic value as a psychological inducer of behavior change.

Play Therapy. A technique or therapy often used with children involving play (usually with toys) to facilitate communication as well as behavior change.

Punishment. In behavior therapy, a consequence of inappropriate behavior; negative reinforcement that immediately follows an inappropriate response for the purpose of decreasing the occurrence of the response.

Puppet Therapy. A technique of counseling that employs play puppets, usually with children, in order to facilitate communication, imitation, expression, and therapy or counseling in general.

Questioning. A verbal technique in counseling which is simply an interrogative statement requiring an open-ended or closed- ended answer from the client.

Rape Counseling. Counseling victims in regards to the prevention of rape and/or adjustment subsequent to rape; methods employed include role playing, rape simulation, supportive techniques, and audio-visual presentation (such as film).

Rapport. Refers to the tone of the counseling relationship which is characterized by a relaxed state, harmony, warmth, naturalness, ease in verbal exchange, and mutual acceptance between the counselor and the client.

Rational-Emotive Therapy (RET). A counseling/psychotherapy theory that emphasizes rational thinking as a goal of counseling; it is associated with Albert Ellis.

Reality Therapy. A counseling theory founded by William Glasser; it focuses on responsibility, needs of the client, identity, and current behavior.

Reassurance. A verbal counseling technique that provides support and comfort to the client in a moment of difficulty and suffering.

Reciprocal Inhibition. The inhibition, elimination, or weakening of an old response by the introduction of a new one; also a theory of counseling and psychotherapy associated with Joseph Wolpe and based on the principles of learning theory, especially principles of classical conditioning.

Recreational Therapy. The applied use of recreation or games for the therapeutic benefit of the client.

Referral. A technique involving the process of transferring the client to another professional or program for special assistance or services.

Reflection. A verbal technique in which the counselor reflects the feeling or content of what the client is communicating; a technique associated with Carl Rogers' client-centered therapy.

Relaxation Therapy. A step in Joseph Wolpe's systematic desensitization process; in general, techniques used to reduce tension, usually muscle tension. (Instructions for relaxation techniques are available in programmed form on cassette audio-tapes and phonograph records.)

Release Therapy. A short-term therapy often practiced with children of traumatic experience in order to allow them a means of expressing repressed emotions related to their trauma.

Role Playing. A technique wherein the client assumes a role or character, other than his or her own, in acting out a scene or playlet for the purpose of better understanding self and relationships with others.

Role Reversal. A role-playing technique whereby the client is requested to play a role opposite to his or her own natural behavior (e.g., an assertive role vs. a submissive role); the client may also play the role of another person he/she knows or switch roles with another person in a dyadic role-playing situation within a group setting.

Role Taking. In group counseling, a method in which group members examine the interactions among themselves and begin to recognize members by their behavioral actions and identities.

Screening. A diagnostic interview in order to determine a person's readiness or acceptability for group counseling or a special guidance activity.

Script Analysis (or Analysis of Scripts). In transactional analysis, a technique of analyzing and restructuring scripts via group therapy, advanced groups, and dreams; the goal of analysis of scripts is to alter the ineffective script or transcend it by substituting a new script with a more active "adult."

Self-Exploration. The client's exploration of feelings and attitudes via the therapeutic facilitation of the counselor.

Self-Help Groups. Groups with members who support each other in eliminating a problem or resolving an issue that is common to all of them; examples of self-help groups include Alcoholics Anonymous and Weight Watchers.

Sensitivity Training. Has reference to growth groups or human relations training groups including T-groups, encounter groups, confrontation groups, and marathon groups.

Sexuality Therapy. Laboratory techniques for the purposes of resolving sexual inadequacies of sexual partners or of one partner in a sexual dyad; also refers to any counseling related to sexuality or sexual adjustment.

Shaping. In learning theory, a technique of creating a new behavioral response by initially reinforcing any response that resembles the desired behavioral response; also referred to as successive approximation.

Sharing Hunches. In group Gestalt therapy, a technique whereby group members are encouraged to share their feelings or perceptions of others and others' problems in the form of "hunches" (e.g., "It is my hunch that you...").

Shuttle Technique. A technique in Gestalt therapy whereby the client's attention is shuttled back and forth between two topics or two activities for the purpose of facilitating awareness.

Silence. A brief period of no verbal exchange in counseling; a technique used in counseling for the purpose of encouraging talk or further elaboration on a topic by the client; also a long pause during the counseling session.

Sociodrama. A group technique employing role playing for the purpose of helping persons to understand and clarify social factors that influence human behavior; it is also employed to teach socially appropriate behavior; associated with the work of J. L. Moreno.

Sociometry. A technique used to measure or assess interpersonal preferences among members of a group as related to a given personality criterion (e.g., "Who do you *like* the best and second best in your class?").

Spectator Therapy. Therapy in which a client learns by observing the behavior of live or symbolic models; also used interchangeably with modeling or imitative therapy.

"Stop" Technique. A technique that employs the therapist's exclamatory and repeated verbalization of the word "stop" in the presence of a client's thought of an undersirable idea or image in order to eliminate the thought.

Story-Book Counseling. A group technique with children wherein a story is read for the purpose of getting pupils to identify with characters and to discuss characters and symbols in the story as related to their own life concerns.

Structuring. Refers to setting limits and guidelines for the counseling relationship; limits are often defined in terms of time, role, and behavioral actions.

Suggestion. A mild form of advice giving; a verbal technique in counseling.

Summarizing. A verbal technique in counseling that is employed to pull together and put into perspective relevant material shared by the client during the counseling session; a brief summation of the theme or important points of a counseling session.

Supervision. A one-to-one learning process whereby an experienced counselor or counselor educator provides meaningful feedback and structuring to a counselor-in-training; a quasi-peer relationship in which an experienced counselor or therapist helps a junior colleague to self-learn through practice.

Supportive Therapy. A form of therapy that uses a variety of supportive and motivational techniques such as reassurance, suggestion, persuasion, and advice.

Symptomatic Therapy. In eclectic counseling, refers to a variety of treatment methods and therapeutic techniques employed in order to eliminate or relieve behavior symptoms of the client; symptoms that are often immediate and necessary to remove before facilitating further treatment.

Synanon. A group approach for the counseling of drug addict; it often employs confrontation as a major technique.

Systematic Counseling. A theory of counseling emphasizing the systems approach to counseling or a blueprint of counseling steps based on each client's problem and needs; flow-charts are presented in explaining the movement of the client through various alternative points within a system.

Systematic Desensitization. A counterconditioning process; a technique of weakening the response to an unpleasant stimulus by gradually introducing an incompatible (pleasant) stimulus; a technique that is associated with Joseph Wolpe.

Systemic Counseling. A theory of counseling that emphasizes changing the dominant White system in order to meet the needs of Blacks and resolve racial conflict that interferes with the adjustment and growth of Blacks; it views the counselor as an advocate and agent of change; associated with T. Gunnings and G. Simpkins.

Task-Oriented Group. A group with a specific problem to solve or an assigned task on which to work.

Tentative Analysis. A partial diagnosis in which the counselor cautiously presents various possible causes of a problem while allowing for the client's reactions and feedback on each.

Termination. Has reference to terminating a counseling relationship or a counseling session; also relates to techniques employed in effectively terminating counseling.

T-Group. Represents the term "training-group"; a form of growth group that focuses on interpersonal effectiveness and personal growth; originated as an NTL, leaderless, sensitivity group.

Thermotherapy. A treatment of human disorders by raising the temperature of the body.

Time-Out. A technique of temporarily removing the person, especially child or infant, from a behavioral setting or from reinforcers that serve to enhance or maintain an unwanted behavior such as a temper tantrum.

Timing. Has reference to an appropriate time in the counseling relationship for the counselor's use of a technique, strategy, or reinforcement event in order to facilitate insight or action on the part of the client.

Token Economy. In behavior modification or learning theory, the use of tokens to reinforce a specific behavior; the tokens are later exchanged for a valued reward (a back-up reinforcer) or a choice from a variety of rewards.

Total Push Therapy. Associated with Abraham Myerson, a comprehensive approach that vigorously applies a variety of therapeutic techniques to the overall treatment of the client or patient.

Trait-and-Factor Counseling (or Trait-Factor). A theory of counseling popularized by E.G. Williamson and sometimes referred to as directive counseling, the Minnesota point of view, or counselor-centered therapy; it focuses on assessing behavioral traits of the client in relationship to educational and career placement as well as social adjustment.

Transactional Analysis (TA). A theory of counseling and psychotherapy focusing on interpersonal conflict and development and employing the concepts of scripts, games, and ego states (parent, adult, and child); associated with Eric Berne.

Transcendental Meditation (TM). A form of meditation popularized in the Western world by Maharishi Mahesh Yogi; the process involves concentration on an assigned sound that has no meaning but which serves to facilitate subtle levels of thought, deep relaxation, and improved awareness.

Transcendent Counseling. A theory of counseling that deals with changing the lifestyle of the person; it involves interpersonal counseling as well as treatment through training activities such as meditation, exercises, relaxation training, nutritional orientation, and growth groups; associated with F. Harper and W. Stone.

Transference Analysis. A technique of using transference in the counseling relationship as a means of making the client aware of the motives, causes, and dynamics of his or her relationships; a technique associated with psychoanalytic theory.

Trust Exercise. In growth groups, a nonverbal exercise or technique in which one group member tests his or her trust of the group by standing in the center of a small circle of standing members and falling limply into the supportive hand of the group (sometimes being pushed around the group from member to member while not being allowed to fall); another version involves a dyad whereby one member falls backwards into the arms of a second person who is entrusted to catch and protect the falling individual.

Tutorial Counseling. A process or concept developed by Frederick Thorne; it focuses on teaching the client to understand self in the functioning environment and to acquire skills for improving situational adjustment.

Unfinished Business. A concept related to psychoanalytic theory as well as Gestalt therapy; it refers to the client's discussion of past experiences that affect present behavior or the discussion of feelings that are denied awareness and acceptance; also the discussion of unresolved conflict and feelings.

Unfinished Story. A guidance technique with children wherein an unfinished story is completed via role playing, discussion, or writing; it stimulates identification, personal information about the pupil's concerns, and dialogue.

Unfreezing. In group work, refers to freeing the individual from rigid beliefs and long-held perceptions of self, others, and the world.

Values Clarification. Training or exercises to help the client become more aware of his/her values and how these values affect daily living and decision-making; also refers to a seven-step approach for processing beliefs and values through structured exercises. (See Louis Raths, et al. *Values and Teaching*; also Sidney B. Simon, et al. *Values Clarification: A Handbook of Practical Strategies for Teachers and Students.*)

Videotherapy. The use of video playback, film, and other video techniques in order to facilitate modeling, role playing, sex therapy, behavioral rehearsal, assertiveness training, and a number of other therapeutic processes.

Wellness. A recent movement in medicine and health counseling that emphasizes healthy lifestyles, prevention of illness, and self-treatment.

"What If" Technique. A technique used to get the client to project, imagine, or explore what it would be like if he or she could attain desired wishes, feelings, or behaviors.

Will Therapy. Associated with Otto Rank; a therapy that focuses on psychological independence from the womb, a self-determining lifestyle, and assertiveness.

Working Through. A psychoanalytic technique or process that refers to the therapist's facilitating the client's movement toward insight, exploration of in-depth feeling, understanding of transference relations, and connecting of past and present; it is more evident and appropriate in the latter phase of the therapy relationship.

Yoga. A form of meditation involving mental and physical exercises or techniques in order to alter one's state of consciousness; often employed to gain self-control, a sense of calm, and self-liberation. The different yoga techniques include breathing exercises, body-position exercises, and concentration on various parts of one's body.

BIBLIOGRAPHY

(Recent Books on Techniques & Theories of Counseling)

Atkinson, D.R., & Morten, G. (1983). *Counseling American minorities: A cross-cultural perspective* (2nd ed.). Dubuque, IA: Wm. C. Brown.

Axelson, J.A. (1985). *Counseling and development in a multicultural society.* Monterey, CA: Brooks/Cole.

Becvar, D.S., & Becvar, R.J. (1988). *Family therapy: A systemic integration.* Boston: Allyn & Bacon.

Belkin, G.S. (1987). *Contemporary psychotherapies* (2nd ed.). Monterey, CA: Brooks/Cole.

Bellack, A.S., & Hersen, M. (1985). *Dictionary of behavior therapy techniques.* New York: Pergamon.

Benjamin, A. (1987). *The helping interview: With case illustrations (4th ed.).* Boston: Houghton Mifflin.

Beutler, L.E. (1983). *Eclectic psychotherapy: A systematic approach.* New York: Pergamon.

Blechman, E.A., & Brownell, K.D. (Eds.). (1988). *Handbook of behavioral medicine for women.* New York: Pergamon.

Brammer, L.M. (1988). *The helping relationship: Process and skills.* Englewood Cliffs, NJ: Prentice-Hall.

Brody, C.M. (1987). *Women's therapy groups.* New York: Springer.

Burke, J.F. (1989). *Contemporary approaches to psychotherapy and counseling: The self-regulation and maturity model.* Monterey, CA: Brooks/Cole.

Carkhuff, R.R. (1987). *The art of helping VI* (6th ed.). Amherst, MA: Human Resource Development Press.

Corey, G. (1986). *A case approach to counseling and psychotherapy* (2nd ed.). Monterey, CA: Brooks/Cole.

Corey, G. (1986). *Theory and practice of counseling and psychotherapy* (3rd ed.). Monterey, CA: Brooks/Cole.

Corey, G., & Corey, M.S. (1987). *Groups: Process and practice* (3rd ed.). Monterey, CA: Brooks/Cole.

Corey, G., Corey, M.S., Callanan, P.J., & Russell, J.M. (1988). *Group techniques* (rev. ed.). Monterey, CA: Brooks/Cole.

Corey, M.S., & Corey, G. (1989). *Becoming a helper*. Monterey, CA: Brooks/Cole.

Dalley, T. (Ed.). (1984). *Art as therapy: An introduction to the use of art as a therapeutic technique*. New York: Routledge.

Drapela, V.J. (1983). *Counselor as consultant and supervisor*. Springfield, IL: Charles C. Thomas.

Egan, G. (1986). *Exercises in helping skills (a training manual to accompany the s skilled helper)* (3rd ed.). Monterey, CA: Brooks/Cole.

Egan, G. (1986). *The skilled helper: A systematic approach to effective helping* (3rd ed.). Monterey, CA: Brooks/Cole.

Ellis, A., & Dryden, W. (1987). *The practice of rational-emotive therapy*. New York: Springer.

Ellis, A., McInerney, J.F., DiGuiseppe, R., & Yeager, R.J. (1988). *Rational- Emotive therapy with alcoholics & substance abusers*. New York: Pergamon.

Evans, D. R., Hearn, M.T., Uhlemann, M.R., & Ivey, A.E. (1989). *Essential interviewing: A programmed approach to effective communication* (3rd ed.). Monterey, CA: Brooks/Cole.

Everett, C.A. (Ed.). (1985). *Divorce mediation: Perspectives on the field*. New York: Haworth.

Eysenck, H.J., & Martin, I. (Eds.). (1987). *Theoretical foundations of behavior therapy*. New York: Plenum.

Gazda, G.M. (1984). *Group counseling: A developmental approach* (3rd ed.). Boston: Allyn & Bacon.

George, R.L., & Dustin, D. (1988). *Group counseling: Theory and practice*. Englewood Cliffs, NJ: Prentice-Hall.

Hersen, M., & Bellack, A.S. (Eds.). (1988). *Dictionary of behavioral assessment techniques*. New York: Pergamon.

Hersen, M., & Last, C.G. (1985). *Behavior therapy casebook*. New York: Springer.

Hershenson, D.B., & Power, P.W. (1987). *Mental health counseling: Therapy and practice*. New York: Pergamon.

Hester, R.K., & Miller, W.R. (Eds.). (1988). *Handbook of alcoholism treatment approaches: Effective alternatives.* New York: Pergamon.

Hummel, D.L., Talbutt, L.C., & Alexander, M.D. (1985). *Law and ethics in counseling.* New York: Van Nostrand Reinhold.

Ivey, A.E. (1988). *Intentional interviewing and counseling: Facilitating client development* (2nd ed.). Monterey, CA: Brooks/Cole.

Jacobs, E.E., Harvill, R.L., & Masson, R.L. (1988). *Group counseling: Strategies and skills.* Monterey, CA: Brooks/Cole.

Kanfer, F.H., & Goldstein, A.P. (1986). *Helping people change: A textbook of methods* (3rd ed.). New York: Pergamon.

Kazdin, A.E. (1988). *Child psychotherapy: Developing and identifying effective treatments.* New York: Pergamon.

Kottler, J.A., & Brown, R.W. (1985). *Introduction to therapeutic counseling.* Monterey, CA: Brooks/Cole.

Lakin, M. (1985). *The helping group: Therapeutic principles and issues.* New York: Pergamon.

Mackey, R.C., Hughes, J.R., & Carver, E.J. (Eds.). (1989). *Empathy in the helping relationship.* New York: Springer.

Maultsby, M.C., Jr. (1984). *Rational behavior therapy.* Englewood Cliffs, NJ: Prentice-Hall.

Meier, S.T. (1989). *Elements of counseling.* Monterey, CA: Brooks/Cole.

Napier, R.W., & Gershenfeld, M. (1985). *Groups: Theory and experience* (3rd ed.). Boston: Houghton Mifflin.

Napier, R.W., & Gershenfeld, M. (1985). *Making groups work: A guide for group leaders.* Boston: Houghton Mifflin.

Nicholson, J.A., & Golsan, G. (1983). *The creative counselor.* New York: McGraw-Hill.

Ohlsen, M.M., Horne, A.M., & Lawe, C.F. (1988). *Group counseling* (3rd ed.). New York: Holt, Rinehart & Winston.

Okun, B.F. (1987). *Effective helping: Interviewing and counseling techniques* (3rd ed.). Monterey, CA: Brooks/Cole.

Osipow, S.H., Walsh, W.B., & Tosi, D.J. (1984). *A survey of counseling methods* (rev. ed.). Homewood, IL: Dorsey.

Patterson, C.H. (1985). *The therapeutic relationship: Foundations for an eclectic psychotherapy.* Monterey, CA: Brooks/Cole.

Patterson, C.H. (1986). *Theories of counseling and psychotherapy* (4th ed.). New York: Harper & Row.

Pietrofesa, J., Hoffman, A.M., & Splete, H. (1984). *Counseling: An ntroduction.* Boston: Houghton Mifflin.

Sachs, M.L., & Buffone, G.W. (Eds.). (1984). *Running as therapy: An integrated approach.* Lincoln, NE: University of Nebraska Press.

Schwartz, M.S., & Associates (1987). *Biofeedback: A practitioner's guide .* New York: Guilford.

Thompson, C.L., & Rudolph, L.B. (1988). *Counseling children* (2nd ed.). Monterey, CA: Brooks/Cole.

Weiss, L. (1986). *Dream analysis in psychotherapy.* New York: Pergamon.

Wolpe, J. (1982). *The practice of behavior therapy* (3rd ed.). New York: Pergamon.

Yalom, I.D. (1985). *Theory and practice of group psychotherapy* (3rd ed.). New York: Basic Books.

INDEX

concepts, 27
goals, 27
techniques, 28
observations and evaluation, 28-29

F

Follow-Up, 130-132

G

Gestalt therapy
proponent, 29
assumptions, 30
concepts, 31
goals, 31
techniques, 32
observations and evaluation, 32-33
Group counseling
goals and outcomes, 159
Groups
basic concepts, 153
models, 155
starting, 158
techniques and exercises, 165
therapeutic & antitherapeutic
forces, 162

H

Hispanics, 186, 188, 192
Hypnosis, 139-141

I

Information giving, 72-75
Interest inventories, 111-113
Interpersonal skills training, 138-139
Interpretation
definitions, 64
purposes and outcomes, 64
applications, 64-65
examples of, 65-66
Interview, 105-108

L

Listening, 93-94

M

Music theapy, 146-147

N

Nonverbal behavior
definitions, 89
examples of, 89-91
Non-White ethnicities, 186-193

P

Paralinguistic cues
definition, 92
examples of 92-93
Personality tests
definition, 113
projective, 113
objective, 113
expressive movement, 114
functions of, 114
Person-Centered therapy
(see client-centered therapy)
Photocounseling
definition, 98
process, 98
outcomes, 98-99
applications, 99
Poetry therapy
definition, 148
methods and techniques, 148
examples of, 149-150
Probing, 85
Proposal writing, 182-185
Psychoanalysis
proponent, 34
assumptions, 34-35
concepts, 35-36
goals, 36
techniques of, 36-37
observations and evaluation, 37-38
Psychotherapy